Don't Cook the Goose that Lays the Golden *Retirement* Eggs

STRAIGHTFORWARD STRATEGIES
TO HELP PROTECT YOUR NEST EGG

Scott Carter, RICP®, CRPC®

Financial Security Alliance

HAMPDEN, MAINE

Scott Carter/Financial Security Alliance
1088 Western Avenue
Hampden, ME 04444
https://fsaincomesolutions.com

Book layout ©2013 BookDesignTemplates.com

Don't Cook the Goose that Lays the Golden Retirement Eggs/ Scott Carter. — 1st ed.
ISBN 978-1542635318

Contents

Dedicated to my wife, Lisa

"Without counsel, plans go awry. But in the multitude of counselors they are established."

—PROVERBS 15:22

PREFACE

L et me start this book by asking you the following question. What if it were possible that you actually owned a magical goose that laid golden eggs just for you? Take a second and really think about that. You no longer work; you are totally dependent on what that goose will produce for you. Now, let me ask you a question, what would you do to protect that goose?

You most likely would feed your goose the healthiest, most high-quality food you could find. The goose would live luxuriously in a temperature-controlled home. Perhaps we could find the eggs on large, soft cushions covered in pure, soft silk. Of course, the environment the goose lived in would have state-of-the-art security. In other words, you would do whatever you could to keep that goose safe and secure. Wouldn't you?

I would like you to think of your retirement funds as that goose. It could take 30 to 40 years to grow this nest egg, or this Golden Goose, that will be responsible for taking care of you for the next 20, 30 or even 40 years in retirement. It took a lot of time, effort and struggle to grow this little gosling into the goose it is today.

Think back to when you first started working. My first job was on a local farm. Several of my friends and I got jobs during the summer working long hours every day. Literally from sunrise to sunset. It was the first summer I gave up going to the lake with my family. I had a bigger goal than having fun at the lake. It was the summer that I was old enough to get my license. All I could dream about was earning enough money to buy a car. To me, having my own car meant my first taste of independence and freedom. My parents had already informed me that with the purchase of a car came additional responsibilities like car maintenance and gas. In my 15-year-old-mind, the added responsibility was well worth having my own wheels.

I worked all that summer and after school, Monday through Saturday, for about 10 months before my parents thought I had enough money saved up to begin my car search. Let me tell you, my first car was no prize to most people, but I had earned the money that purchased the car, and what a great feeling that was! I will never forget the first time I rolled into the school yard in my blue four-speed, four-door, bucket-seated Dodge Colt. That car lasted for years to come; in fact, it got me through college.

I was fortunate to have parents who taught me to save a portion of what I earned. I always had a savings account, lean as it might have been at times. However, even with the great guidance I had, it never occurred to me to save for retirement.

Most of you would agree that saving for retirement was the last thing on your minds when you were young. For many of us, we were more interested in buying that sporty car to go riding around in with our friends. At that point in our lives we all firmly believed that age 50 was ancient and was a long, long time away.

Yet, before we knew it, we were in the next phase of our lives, where we found that special person, got married and started a family. Once the kids started arriving and life was not quite so carefree, we began to reassess things. This was when we began to change our thinking about age 50 being old. I think it must have been my generation that came up with the idea that 50 is the new 30, 60 is the new 40 and 70 is the new 50. I couldn't agree more.

It is usually at this point many of us start thinking about planning for retirement. Some of us might want to save and retire like our parents did, or perhaps we witnessed a lack of planning and don't want to struggle as our parents did in retirement. So we start making our retirement and savings plans and then something gets in the way.... LIFE! I am confident that you are nodding with agreement at this statement. Perhaps you might even give a sigh or two. Life gets in the way and our best laid plans get a little off track at times. There are doctor's bills, clothes, food, car repairs, insurance premiums, mortgage payments, braces for teeth, books for school, the second car, the sports equipment, the third car (for the child this time, who promised to pay you back!), the college tuition, graduations, weddings and on and on it goes.

But somehow it all seems to work out and you get to the time in your life where you start thinking seriously about retirement, and not just as a distant eventuality. Your retirement account may not be as big as you dreamed, but you have sacrificed and done the best you could to build what you have. At this point you hope and pray it is enough.

Over your working years you "fed" your little gosling (retirement account) and did the best you could to protect it. Before you know it, the day you thought would never come is here: Retirement! Now something has changed with your little gosling; it has matured to a full-grown goose and is capable of laying the golden eggs that will take care of you in retirement! So, now what are you going to do, have a goose barbecue? Make goose stew? Of course not! You wouldn't even think about cooking this goose, it's too valuable, right? *Or would you?*

I will talk more about how we could be putting ourselves in jeopardy of doing just that in later chapters, and what my idea of adding "goose insurance" to the portfolio looks like. When I talk about goose insurance, I am talking about conservative strategies you can use to help protect your assets from being devastated by poor returns or sharp downturns in the stock market, as we have seen in previous years such as 2008. Among other examples, in Chapter 7 I will show you an example of a portfolio that would have lost 19 percent based on the S&P 500 stock market index during the years of 2000 to 2009. But, after adding more conservative strategies in the same period of time, the same portfolio would have *increased* by 12 percent. Goose insurance at work!

As we all know, with the upheaval of economic markets, the roller coaster ride of the stock market, and 10,000 baby boomers turning 65 every day, it is more important than ever not to "cook the goose" that lays the golden retirement eggs. I have been in the investment advisory business for well over 30 years now, and in that time I have witnessed many bad decisions that have *cooked the goose.* There are many ways people cook their retirement goose. Retiring too young, not being on the same page with your spouse, loaning large sums of money to family members and not being paid back, and having too much risk in the retirement portfolio are just a few of the reasons people fail to protect their retirement goose. Typically, these decisions have been made without taking the time to truly have a plan, one that is set in stone to protect you from many of the possible failures listed above. A plan that would make sure your golden-egg-laying goose is safe and cared for to carry you through your golden years.

In the following chapters, I am going to share with you the basic principles of retirement income planning. Will they *all* apply to you? Maybe, maybe not, but my hope is that you will be able to use one or more of these strategies to either set up your initial retirement plan, adjust the plan you already have, or pass along the ideas to someone who has not started the process yet.

This book is written for those people whom I refer to as being in the "Retirement Danger Zone." This is a period of time that is approximately 10 years before one's retirement date, as well as the first 10 years into retirement. This is a very critical period of time, when our financial decisions could make or break our financial futures.

Some topics this book will cover:

- Plans to build a reliable income into your retirement, or what I often refer to as mailbox money.
- How much risk someone should take in retirement.
- How to perform a "portfolio stress test."
- How to properly coordinate retirement assets and Social Security income to maximize both.
- How to navigate the Retirement Danger Zone.
- How to make sure you don't cook the goose that lays your golden retirement eggs (goose insurance!).

To help you build confidence that you are retaining the information, I have also included quizzes throughout the book.

My Own Story

AND WHY I AM INTERESTED IN YOUR FUTURE

M y wife and I share many passions, including our professional work as financial advisors. Likewise, we share reasons for dedicating ourselves to this pursuit. I would like to share one that is very personal to me and was the primary motivation for starting my own business focusing on the retirement income planning aspect. I wish it was a positive story; unfortunately, it wasn't. In fact, it was a story that impacted most of my mother's retirement years, or what should have been her retirement years. My parents made an uninformed financial decision that had devastating consequences, causing my mother to struggle financially for the rest of her life.

My father was a dedicated employee who worked very hard for many years at a local paper mill. My father worked many long hours, oftentimes working the graveyard shift to get the extra pay to provide for our family. He worked hard so my mother could do the job she always wanted to do: the job of staying home to raise her three boys. Finally, the day came when my mother and father decided they could begin to enjoy their retirement years together. My brothers and I were all grown and because of my father's many years at the mill, he had a nice retirement account for him and my mother to finally enjoy. The day of my father's retirement was a joyous one. His co-workers and friends gave him a retirement party, acknowledging all my father's accomplishments throughout his long career. It was a happy time for my parents. They finally were going to have the time and money to enjoy their little home on the lake and even get some traveling in.

For the first year of their retirement, life was as they had dreamed. Many days you would find them with their two dogs at the lake. It didn't matter if it was summer or winter, they loved being at the lake. If you are not from the Northeast, you may not realize how much snow we get in the winter and how bitterly cold it is. I think that was when my parents enjoyed the lake the most, however. You would find them with a roaring fire in the wood stove, ice fishing traps all set on the lake, coffee percolating on the stove and something hearty and warm simmering for guests who might show up to join them. They were living the retirement they had always dreamed of.

However, my father died unexpectedly about one year after he retired, shattering their dream. The loss of a father and husband at such a young age was heartbreaking and scary at the same time to us. My mother not only lost her dearest friend, she also had to somehow pick up the pieces and take care of all the things my father had been doing. We all knew how much our lives would change without my father, especially for my mother. At least she would be okay financially — she would have my father's pension to help take care of her. ... Or so she thought.

The day my mother went in to talk with the human resources department at the mill is etched into my mind forever. My mother assumed this was an appointment to simply change the pension check from my father's name to hers. However, that was not the case at all. My mother was told at that meeting that she would not be able to collect my father's pension because of the choice they made when he retired. They had selected "full retirement benefits," which meant the company would pay no survivor's benefits to her. My parents really had no idea of the impact of that decision. They simply chose the largest monthly payout without fully realizing what it would mean if something happened to my father. Imagine being in that room, in her shoes, getting that news; how would you feel? My mother was devastated, as I think most people would be.

As the youngest of three boys, I will never forget her words. She said to us, "I am not going to get his pension, what am I going to do?" She was panicked because this was life-changing news for her, and it wasn't good news. Because of this one uninformed decision, my mother was forced into a very different lifestyle. She was accustomed to being at home, raising the children and running a household. She was now forced to find a job, downsize, sell the beloved lake home she had shared for years with the love of her life, and lower her standard of living. To help my mother, there were many times my brothers and I would anonymously pay her property taxes or fill her oil tank. My mother was determined that her children would not pay her bills, so we had the oil company fill her tank when she wasn't there and send the slip to one of us, circumventing her knowledge entirely. She always assumed her property taxes just stayed low and affordable, for which she was very thankful. Needless to say, her life COMPLETELY changed! Her dreams of retirement vanished the day she was told that the one choice they made for my father's pension was one that left her fending for herself.

Being a strong woman, she managed to survive, but she could never replace the monetary value that the lost pension would have provided. She struggled financially for the rest of her life.

This early life experience spurred me to help as many people as I possibly could, hoping to spare others the pain that might be caused by such uninformed financial decisions. I had a vision to have my own independent practice where I could take the necessary time with each person to make sure they understood the impact of the decisions they were making and the possible pitfalls they could face as a result of each different decision they might make.

My business partner and I have owned our own financial advisory practice for many years now. I would like to share with you how I met her.

Approximately 25 years ago, I was working in an office complex that I shared with a few other financial advisors. At that time, we had a tech room that had several computers for research and studying. As I opened the door to the tech room, I saw the most beautiful woman I had ever seen studying on one of the computers. She took my breath away and I distinctly remember thinking right then and there, "This is the girl I am going to marry." Her name was Lisa and she was a nurse who was studying for her financial licenses, leaving her career as a nurse to become a financial advisor. When I asked her why she would leave nursing to become a financial advisor, she explained how much she loved educating and helping people. She believed that one of the most important things she could do was use these passions to help people with their finances, enabling them to live independent, comfortable, successful lives to the best of their ability. She had witnessed too many people making poor decisions for different reasons that left them financially devastated.

Because of our shared beliefs and values, Lisa and I quickly became great friends. Five years after first seeing her in that computer room, I got my courage up to ask her to be my wife, and she said, "Yes." We have been happily married ever since and have been blessed to work together in our financial services practice.

In 1984, at the "ripe old age" of 24, I decided to start working in the financial services industry. I started out working part time in an apprenticeship while studying for my licenses and exams. I loved helping people, and I witnessed what a difference informed planning could make in their lives. I worked for a large firm in an apprenticeship position for approximately six years. As my experience grew and the focus of my practice turned more to retirement income planning, I realized the company I was with did not have the resources available to allow me to fully pursue income planning like I wanted. The company's focus was primarily on providing mutual funds and a limited line of insurance products. I felt like this made it very difficult to do the right job for my clients. As an independent minded advisor, I felt it was necessary to have the whole world of financial products available to choose from.

So, in 1990, my wife Lisa — who wholeheartedly shared my vision — and I decided to branch out on our own, which was when our income planning practice started and Financial Security Alliance, Inc. was born. Since then, I have gone on to achieve the Retirement Income Certified Professional® designation through The American College of Financial Services and the Chartered Retirement Planning Counselor℠ designation through The College for Financial Planning, and currently help hundreds of clients avoid potential retirement pitfalls so they can enjoy a stable retirement. As an Investment Advisor Representative and income planner, I believe it is critical to be totally independent so I can make the right decisions for clients without a company telling me which products to use. My motto is: "Plan first, product second."

Over the years, we have developed certain processes and tools designed to help people avoid the unintended consequences of a bad financial decision. For instance, as pension strategies are near to my heart, we help those who have pensions make their initial pension decisions. Most people who have a pension will have anywhere from eight to 10 or more options to choose from, and the paperwork can get very confusing. Typically, we see options that range from a single life payout (which usually carries the highest monthly payments), to many combinations of survivor benefit options, such as 100 percent survivor, 75 percent survivor and 50 percent survivor options. These survivor options will have reduced monthly payouts according to how much of the benefit is left to the survivor. Also, many pensions have a lump sum rollover option that will allow the retiree to roll over the lump sum to his or her own IRA. They can then build their own income from these funds, or — if they have other financial resources such as income from a part-time job after they retire — they can let this lump sum grow for future income or for liquid cash purposes.

This initial decision is very important; if it is made incorrectly, the consequences could be devastating in the future. For example, if a couple chooses the single life option and the retiree passes away soon after making this decision, in most pensions, the income stops. The spouse might receive some very devastating news. This is exactly what happened in my mother's situation.

This is an area of our practice that my wife and I really bond over. Helping people understand the importance of these decisions and avoid these negative consequences is at the heart of our practice.

I hope by writing this book I can pass along some of the wisdom and strategies I have learned over these many years. In some way, I hope to help you achieve the retirement you have always dreamed of having without having to face the possible heartache that comes from making the wrong decision because you were not informed of all your choices.

CHAPTER 2

Are Things Complicated Today?

How about electronics? The phone I carry on my belt is many times smaller, is more powerful, and can perform more tasks than my first desktop computer! Things have changed so rapidly in this area that it becomes very difficult to keep up with technology, would you agree? When I was leaving high school, computers were just becoming part of the curriculum. So for me, computers and all the technology that goes along with them were not second nature. I literally hired high school computer teachers to come to my office to train myself and my staff on all the technology as it was quickly advancing.

Is retirement planning complicated? It sure can be with the vast array of strategies, investments and even opinions from the army of financial planners and brokers out there. One broker might use the "buy and hold" method, which says you should have all your money in the stock market and never move it no matter what happens (sometimes referred to as the "buy and hope" method). Another broker might suggest putting everything in bonds or annuities to keep the principal safe, and another broker might be somewhere in between! It's not a surprise that so many people are totally confused about which direction to go when it comes to planning their retirements. It is often stated that most people spend more time planning vacations than the time they spend planning their retirements!

Could all the noise and overload of information marketed out there have anything to do with people being confused? I think so, and remember, a confused mind tends to do nothing, which in itself is a decision, for good or bad.

I have seen many examples of this in my own practice from people who come in for advice. Many people have been bounced around from broker to broker, looking for the answer to their questions, and end up being so confused that they will stop paying attention to anything that pertains to their investments.

Many people get so discouraged that they actually stop opening up their statements for months at a time. They know they are losing money but they don't have the strength to deal with it. They lose sleep worrying about their finances and their futures, but because they can't seem to get the answers and plans that make sense and work specifically for them, they find themselves hoping and praying their *goose will survive.*

When trying to deal with this particular mindset, I always start out with the following statement:

"My working with clients for over 30 years has shown me that a major reason retirement plans and dreams fail is because of fear and indecision that hinders people from making the correct or necessary decisions. Most of the time the reason for their fear and indecision is a lack of knowledge about a topic or situation.

"My job is to find out your dreams and goals for retirement, help you discover whether they are achievable, and provide you with the education to overcome those fears so you can take the necessary action."

I believe that most people, if given the right information, can make a good decision. In my office, we strive to provide a friendly, relaxing environment where people feel comfortable asking questions and learning. It is a successful planning session when my clients leave with knowledge, confidence and a sense of peace about a plan that they fully understand.

If you find yourself in an office where you do not feel comfortable asking questions, or you feel confused with the answers to your questions, it is most likely not the right place to be.

The decisions you make for retirement could be decisions that greatly affect your life either positively or negatively for the next 30 to 40 years. You should make sure they are ones that match up to your dreams and goals.

Creating a financial plan for your retirement does not have to be confusing or complicated. Make sure you understand it and choose an advisor who is willing to take the time it takes to answer all your questions and really listen to what you want. A good test for this is to see who does the most listening at the first appointment. Ask yourself, "How do they know what I want if I haven't even told them yet?"

I know I have done the right job for my client when they tell me that they get it or they understand how the plan works. It is very important for us to realize that there are many people out there who call themselves "advisors," yet they are really anything but that. It is my opinion that most of the time if you are dealing with someone who is not truly independent, you are most likely dealing with someone who is getting their instructions from a sales manager or supervisor who is telling them what to do or worse yet what to sell you. You might be getting the "special of the month" and not really getting the advice that is right for you.

There are basically two standards that everyone working in the financial services industry must meet. One is the "suitability" standard and the other is the "fiduciary" standard. The suitability standard applies to those people who typically work for a brokerage firm or an insurance company as an employee of that company. A lot of times they are in what is called a "captive" position with the company they are with. They are employed by that company as salespeople, so the company's interests come first.

Under the fiduciary standard, the person is typically a Registered Investment Advisor or an Investment Advisor Representative, working in an independent position. An advisor in this situation will usually look at the client's needs more holistically with the overall retirement plan in mind. As a fiduciary, the interest of the client has to come first, not the company.

After being in the financial services industry for over 30 years and being an Investment Advisor Representative myself, I have seen many examples of clients who had a product sold to them without any planning involved. When new clients come into my office for the first time, we go through a discovery process to see what their plan looks like. In most cases, especially if they have not worked with someone who is a true fiduciary, I end up spending a lot of time trying to undo and correct what has been done. The biggest problem I see is the huge discrepancy of their true risk tolerance and the dreams and plans they have for retirement versus how their assets are actually invested.

I recently had a couple come in for their initial discovery meeting and we found out after doing research into their risk tolerance that they were considered to be moderately conservative investors. This meant their assets should be invested in a position where 60 percent of the portfolio would be in a conservative position such as bonds, annuities, cash, etc. with the remaining 40 percent being invested in a diversified mix of stocks. When I looked at their brokerage statement, they were over 90 percent invested in an aggressive stock portfolio! This couple was in their mid- to late 60s and did not want to take anywhere near the risk they were taking. Because they were sold something instead of having any real retirement income planning done, they were in real jeopardy of cooking their retirement goose and they didn't know it! For some reason, the advisor just didn't hear what they wanted for their retirement years.

This is also a good place to prepare you to receive honest advice from a good advisor. Just because you want to retire at a certain age with a certain income does not mean that you have the assets to do so. Beware of the advisor who does not present a plan to last for your full retirement. Unfortunately, I have seen many clients who are very close to running out of income because the advisor they used just set up the income they wanted in retirement without any plan for longevity.

How much income and how long your money will last with that income amount is a vital part of a successful retirement. There are times when the amount of income you need to retire is just not possible with the amount of money that you have saved for retirement. It is best to know the truth of the matter and not find out years into your retirement, when it most likely will be too late for you to do anything about it.

CHAPTER 3

Things Change, Has Your Perspective?

Y ou may have heard the saying, "You don't know what you don't know until someone points it out to you."

I don't think there is a more true statement. In this time we call the "information age," there is so much noise, chatter and clatter, and so many talking heads all telling us something different; it makes most of our heads spin. However, most of the time, the glut of information thrown at us is useless, especially to our specific lives and circumstances. I think that is why so many of us let it go in one ear and out the other. It is just too much to take it all in.

What I have found in my life is that a single person cannot be an expert in every subject, although I am sure we all know a few people who think they are. I fondly remember my grandparents referring to those people as, "genuine know-it-alls." The older I get, the more I appreciate the simple truths my grandparents taught me. However, I have found one of my most successful strategies is to search out a person who specializes in one area of study and has great references. This should be familiar territory for most of us; after all, you probably have a doctor, a dentist, a car guy, a lawyer and a plumber you prefer. So it is with one's finances. Once you find such an expert, it is essential to ask questions and make sure you fully understand what is being presented. However, remember they most likely know more about the specialty they practice in than your "know-it-all" neighbor or family member might think they know.

When people come in to discuss their retirement goals, an obstacle we face is that many people have unchanging perspectives in an ever-changing world. Although it can be overwhelming at times, it is important for us to be ready to learn new things, especially when they can greatly impact our daily lives.

I am always talking about people needing to be open-minded and willing to learn new things. As I was discussing this with my wife recently, she told me she was pleased to hear that, because she had some new information that she would like to share with me. I then learned that there was a place for my dirty clothes and it was not on the bathroom floor. See, we are constantly learning!

Let's do a little test to see if your perspective has changed over the years.

ATTENTION!!! DO NOT SKIP AHEAD!!! ANSWER EACH QUESTION BEFORE GOING TO THE NEXT PAGE!!!

How many sides does a stop sign have?

What color is a stop sign?

So, how many sides does a stop sign have?
Answer: 8

What color is a stop sign?
Answer: RED

How many sides to a yield sign?

What color is a yield sign?

And how many sides to a yield sign?
Answer: 3

What color is a yield sign?
Answer: RED

Be honest, did you say a yield sign is yellow? If you did, congratulations, you are with the majority of people. It goes to show you the majority is not always right. Now for the real shocker, they stopped making yellow yield signs over 30 years ago. Yield signs are red and white!

This is a great little quiz to show you how things change all around us, but oftentimes our personal perspective doesn't quite keep up.

Decisions we made 20, 30 or even 40 years ago were probably good decisions at the time we made them, but things change and we need to make sure to re-evaluate our decisions with the new information available to us.

My wife is a free spirit and loves new challenges. She is an adventurer at heart. However, she does not do well with too much change, especially all at once. I always remind her that there is one thing we can always count on … things change! To which she responds, "I really don't mind change as long as I am in charge of it." We always get a laugh at this because, as we all know, many times change happens with or without our cooperation.

Take a minute here and think about when you were just graduating from high school. Take a journey down memory lane and think about the changes that have occurred throughout the years of your life so far.

You must remember, as I do, when the telephone was on the wall in the kitchen. Most of our homes had one phone. You had to be home to answer it, and if you weren't there, people had to call back because there was no way to leave a message. How about the television? Most homes had one television and there were four channels available until they signed off at night, and then they didn't have programming until the next morning. Do you remember the national anthem being played, and then the noise of static? Those are just two examples of how drastically things have changed in our lives.

With all this in mind, what transition do you think has been the most significant change in retirement income planning in recent history?

PENSION PLAN TO 401(k)

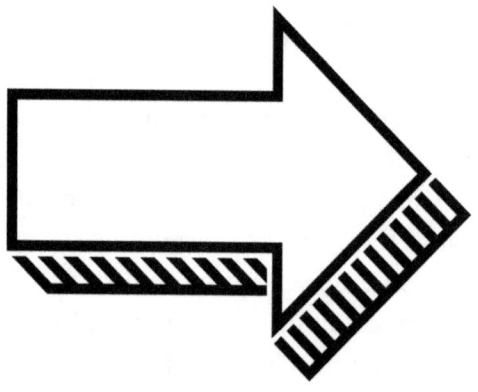

The shift by corporations from the traditional pension plan to the 401(k) has probably had the most significant impact on the retirement income planning process, more than any other change in recent history.

Did you ever hear your parents or grandparents talking about retirement? What did they say? Did they say they were going to roll over their 401(k) and try to live off it for the rest of their lives? Probably not. They most likely said they were going to retire and collect their Social Security, and if they were fortunate enough they would also collect their pension. This is as far as the planning usually went. They were given the amount they would receive from Social Security and, if applicable, their pension as well, and from that information alone they would decide whether it was time to retire or not.

Today, most pensions have been replaced with the 401(k) or 403(b) or a similar qualified plan. This brings up a very important question.

"If we are transitioning from the pension plan to the 401(k), who is responsible for creating your paycheck in retirement?"

YOU ARE!

So, if you are now responsible for creating your own pension, or that *mailbox money* that you can count on receiving every month, doesn't that put you in the role of the planner? Most people trying to decide whether they can retire or if they have to keep on working are not investment advisors or income planners. If your 401(k) or qualified plan is going to be the *goose* that lays your golden eggs to produce the income you need to live on, it is imperative to take the time and work with a professional who will give you an honest assessment prior to helping you make your final decisions.

If the income from the 401(k) is what you will live on for the rest of your life, do you think it is important to get it right? Does retirement income planning become critical? Of course the answer should be a resounding yes!

I mentioned the oft-repeated statement earlier that most people take more time to plan their vacation than they take to plan their retirement.

Imagine that! More time to plan an event that will be over in a few weeks versus planning for a phase in your life that could last 30 years or more. With the recent shift from the traditional pension plan to the 401(k) and other qualified retirement plans, we are put in a position to either do the income planning ourselves or hire someone else to do it for us.

Here I want to pass on what I think is some very sound advice. If your employer offers a 401(k) plan where you work, MAX IT OUT! If you possibly can, you should put the maximum percentage amount into the plan, up to what the company is matching.

For example, if the company is matching your contributions up to 6 percent, make sure you put at least 6 percent of your income into the plan. The company's matching contributions are like getting free money! Why wouldn't you take it? Let's look at a dollars and cents example of this.

Let's say you earn $50,000 per year and you can save 6 percent of your income outside of the 401(k) plan. That would be $3,000 per year and if you did this for 30 years and earned 5 percent interest, you would accumulate over $212,000. If you save the 6 percent of your income in the 401(k) plan and the employer matches what you put away, you would have accumulated more than $424,000. As you can see, if you have the chance to participate in a company plan such as a 401(k), you should. Even if the employer is not matching what you contribute to the plan it is a good idea to still put away what you can into this type of "forced savings" investment plan where the funds are taken out of your paycheck before you actually get the money in your hands. It is a great habit to get into, and most people I have discussed it with say they really don't miss the money once they do it for a while. Savings success rates are a lot higher for people who have their contributions automatically deducted.

CHAPTER 4

I Have Longevity in My Family, So What?

As you have just read, one of the biggest changes in recent history is that the traditional pension plans from most corporations have disappeared and have been replaced by the 401(k), 403(b) and other retirement savings plans, which puts you in the role of creating your retirement income. With life expectancies increasing, some people are living in retirement 30 years or longer and the paycheck that is created from your retirement accounts must last at least that long. Or, to put it another way, that *goose* must be able to deliver those golden eggs to last the rest of your life, and optimally that of the life of your spouse.

Are people really living longer? Let's take a look at recent statistics.[1]

- Most wives will outlive their husbands by about 7 years.
- The chance that one person in a married couple, both age 65, will live to be age 75 is 98.8%.
- The chance that one person in a married couple, both age 65, will live to be age 80 is 95.7%.

---

[1] Calculations based on Society of Actuaries, 2012 Individual Annuity Mortality Tables.

- The chance that one person in a married couple, both age 65, will live to be age 92 is 55.8%.
- The chance that one person in a married couple, both age 65, will live to be age 97 is 25.4%.
- The chance that one person in a married couple, both age 65, will live to be age 100 is 11.9%.

Consider these unique examples of longevity.

- Michelangelo painted the ceiling of the Sistine Chapel at the age of 71.
- George Burns earned his only Academy Award at age 80.
- John Glenn traveled into space at age 77.
- President George H.W. Bush made a parachute jump at age 80.
- Mae Laborde started her acting career at age 93 and acted on television until she died at age 102.
- Buster Martin, who died in 2011 at 105 years old, claimed to have never taken a day off from his plumbing business until the age of 100.
- On her 91st birthday, Lucille Borgen won two events at the 62nd Annual Water Ski National Championships.
- Bill Anderson, a former paratrooper in World War II, completed a coast-to-coast bicycle trek at age 78.
- Nola Ochs became the world's oldest college graduate in 2007 at age 98. She graduated alongside her 21-year-old great-granddaughter.
- George Brunstad is one of the oldest people to swim the English Channel, which he completed shortly after turning age 70.
- At age 63, Mike Melvill became the first private pilot to earn astronaut wings, flying the first privately funded human spaceflight aircraft.

Jeanne Louise Calment holds the record as the oldest fully authenticated age that any human has lived: 122 years, 164 days. At age 85 she took up fencing and at age 100, she was still riding a bike.

Without a doubt, people are living longer. In the classes I teach, I usually ask if anyone knows someone age 90 or above. Without exception, at least one or two of those raising their hands knows someone over the age of 100. It is probable that most of you reading this book also know people over the age of 90 or 100.

My wife definitely has longevity in her family. Her grandmother, who recently passed away, was 98, and her other grandmother is 95 going on 27! She still lives alone, but it is quite difficult to catch her at home. She is on the go all the time.

I personally have a client who just turned 104 years old! He is amazing. This gentleman plays golf two to three times a week and he often walks the course! He goes to Florida every winter (since I live in a cold state, I think this may be his secret to long life!) and has outlived a wife and two girlfriends!

As you can see, the statistics in our country point toward increased longevity. Recently, my wife and I stopped by to visit with our elderly neighbors. As we were sitting around the kitchen table talking, we asked them how everything was going for them. The response they gave was something that should be etched in all our minds as we consider our long-term futures and retirements. They told us that they were getting by, but they were worried about running out of money. My wife and I sympathetically asked them why they were worried about this and they said, "We just never planned on living this long." These neighbors are 87 and 89 years old, and it looks like they have many more years to go.

As an advisor, I ask my clients to explain to me, what is the No. 1 risk that longevity poses?

Most of the time, my clients tell me that it is the risk of outliving their money. They don't want to run out of income in their retirement years. That is a valid concern and one that must be considered when planning for your retirement.

I also have clients or potential clients who sit in my office and tell me they don't want to plan for longevity because they won't live that long, anyway. That is definitely not a sound planning notion and I would be cautious of any advisor who was willing to go along with that idea.

I recently saw a lady in my office who was only 68 and was in a situation where her retirement funds were not going to last for her retirement. I asked her why so much money had been withdrawn at such an early point in her retirement. I found out she had been withdrawing a large monthly income from the retirement account since she was 55. She was still working when she began to withdraw this large monthly amount, but now she wanted to retire. When I asked her why she took such a large monthly income from her retirement funds while she was still working, her response was surprising. "Because the advisor said I could, so I thought, 'Why not?'" "Apparently it was the "why not" that had not been fully discussed and now this woman was facing a serious risk of outliving her retirement income.

I can't express strongly enough that longevity planning should be taken very seriously when considering whether to retire or not.

Another part of the longevity planning puzzle that should seriously be considered is the ever-increasing cost of long-term care. Because people are living longer, the need for long-term care has greatly increased, especially because of cognitive impairment issues such as dementia and Alzheimer's disease.

According to Genworth Financial Inc.'s Annual Cost of Care Survey, in 2016 the national average cost of a semi-private room in a nursing home was $225 per day, or $6,844 per month. A private room was $253 per day, or $7,698 per month. The cost of care in an assisted living facility was $3,628 per month. If home health care is viable, the hourly rate for a home health aide is on average

$125.00 per day. As you can see by these figures, the cost of long-term care can potentially drain an estate quite rapidly. I wish I could write that long-term health care costs were going down and have low inflation, but as you may guess that is not the case. What is the solution?

There are basically three options that most people have, or you could say there are three categories that most people would fit into. The first category is for those people who have enough money saved that they can simply pay their own way in a nursing home, assisted living facility or a home health care situation.

The second category is for those people who just don't have enough money to pay for their care. This group of people will rely on some form of government assistance to pay for their care, either from Medicare, if it is a rehab situation, or from a state-run assistance program.

The third category is the group of people who are kind of "stuck in the middle." These people haven't saved enough money to be able to fully fund their own long-term care costs (or at least not within a comfortable margin) but have saved too much to qualify for state or federal assistance. This group of people usually can benefit from the purchase of long-term-care insurance.

I have heard it said, and in my experience this is true, you buy long-term-care insurance with your health before your dollars. You are not guaranteed long-term-care coverage just because you can afford to pay for it. In most cases, there is strict medical underwriting when applying for long-term-care insurance coverage. Once you pass the medical underwriting portion, then you must decide what coverage is affordable for you. In most cases, the long-term-care insurance would most likely give you partial coverage, while you would pay the balance of the charges incurred. Having at least partial coverage could potentially save you from spending down your assets. In many cases, if planned properly, the partial coverage will allow you to pay the balance using your income instead of directly tapping your retirement assets.

While we're on the subject, I'd like to emphasize that Medicare does not provide coverage for long-term care. Many people are confused about this. Perhaps the confusion is because Medicare covers a limited stay in a rehabilitation facility. The maximum coverage for a rehabilitation stay is usually 100 days. There are also requirements to qualify for this coverage, such as the requirement that you must be able to be rehabilitated through services such as physical and occupational therapy. An easier way to understand this is that you must be able to improve and return home. You will be assessed along the way to see if you are meeting the qualifications to remain in the rehabilitation facility. You are not guaranteed the 100 days of coverage from Medicare or a Medicare Supplement Plan; 100 days is the maximum amount of possible days you could receive coverage for.

Remember that second group of people? The ones whose long-term care is paid for by government programs? Keep in mind that the government doesn't step in until there are no other options. So falling back on those assistance programs is no big deal—as long as you are okay with having to spend all of your assets until there is nothing left for you to have control over, and nothing left to pass to your heirs. Unless your ideal retirement involves being a pauper, longevity and the possibility of long-term care are some very good reasons to consider insuring that Golden Goose.

According to a study done by eldercare.com, a man age 45 and older who is staying in a nursing home has a 79 percent chance of a one- to three-year stay. A female age 45 or older who is staying in a nursing home has a 74 percent chance of a one-to three-year stay. Based on these or similar numbers, we see most people buying at least a three-year coverage period in their long-term-care insurance policies.

In my experience working with long-term-care insurance, if a policy is designed correctly, the premiums can be quite affordable and go a long way in protecting the assets we have all worked so hard to accumulate. I find that in most cases, a couple could pay premiums for 15 to 20 years and still not pay the equivalent of a one-year stay in a nursing care facility. So in effect, we are using smaller dollars today to pay for a larger event down the road.

Let me share a few stories from my practice that might give you a better picture of the importance of at least considering long-term coverage.

This is one of the worst cases that bothers me to this day. Clients of mine, Cleo and Shirley, had long-term-care coverage. They were in their early 80s and enjoying a well-planned, comfortable retirement. As time went on, an in-law that lived close by decided to *help* them take care of their day-to-day tasks such as paying bills. When the bill for their quarterly premium came in for their long-term-care insurance, this in-law argued that they should not pay it and cancel the coverage. She convinced them by telling them that they would never end up in a nursing home because she would take care of them if they ever needed it. I am quite sure she meant this from the bottom of her heart. However, she made a promise she couldn't possibly keep. That very day, the long-term-care insurance company received a call cancelling the policy.

Approximately three months later, Shirley had a severe stroke and was rushed to the hospital. Unfortunately, Shirley did not recover and was left in a vegetative state requiring skilled nursing care in a long-term-care facility. While the family was trying to deal with this tragedy, they quickly realized Cleo was suffering from advanced dementia. Apparently, Shirley had been "covering" for her husband, which is very common; often one spouse works to shield the other's memory lapses from extended family and friends. Nonetheless, Cleo and Shirley spent the remainder of their lives in long-term-care facilities. Shirley passed away 15 months after her stroke and Cleo spent another 18 months in long-term-care before joining his beloved wife. It was always Cleo and Shirley's desire to leave their children an inheritance; however, after the long-term-care expenses, very little was left.

I also had a client for many years, Ellie, who in her late 70s was diagnosed with Alzheimer's. She was never married and had no children. However, she had a brother and sister-in-law that did a great job taking care of her. Eventually, the care became too great for her brother and his wife and they realized Ellie needed to be placed in a long-term-care facility. Ellie had long-term-care coverage, which created many more choices for her care. Because of her long-term-care policy, Ellie was able to have a private room in a very nice facility. Her coverage lasted five years, which covered all but eight months of Ellie's stay. The inheritance Ellie planned to leave to her loved ones was kept intact and her wishes were carried out after her long illness.

Long-term-care insurance is not for everyone and it may not even be available for health reasons, or it may not be affordable, but in my opinion, long-term-care insurance can play a vital role in your attempt to *not cook the goose.*

CHAPTER 5

What Color Is Your Money?

In the finance world, there are basically two types of money, qualified and nonqualified money. What is the difference?

Qualified money is typically money that has been saved in an employer-sponsored plan such as a 401(k), 403(b), corporate pension plan, SEP IRA or traditional IRA outside of the workplace. The No. 1 reason these types of accounts are classified as "qualified" is that taxes have not been paid on the money yet and they qualify for a tax deduction from income. Taxes will come due when the funds are eventually taken out, typically at retirement. With qualified plans, there is a mandate that you must begin withdrawing a required minimum distribution, or RMD, at age 70 ½. This is an important aspect to keep in mind when you are planning your retirement income.

Also, money you withdraw before you are 59 ½ may be subject to a 10 percent federal penalty.

Nonqualified money is typically money that has been saved outside of a retirement plan. Mostly we think of nonqualified money as checking and savings accounts, certificates of deposit (CDs), money market accounts, nonqualified annuities, nonqualified mutual funds and stocks. These funds are classified as nonqualified because you have already paid taxes on the money before you invest it and taxes are paid as the interest is earned in most circumstances, unless it is a tax-deferred annuity.

I also like to break things down a little further into two more categories: What I refer to as Green Money and Red Money.

I categorize Green Money as low risk, or principal-protected, assets.

Red Money I categorize as high risk, or principal-at-risk, assets.

Here is an example of some Green Money assets.

1. Bank CDs
2. Checking accounts
3. Savings accounts
4. Money market accounts
5. Annuities

These assets have some form of principal protection, such as FDIC insurance at the bank. In the case of annuities, the principal protection is backed by the claims-paying ability of the insurance company.

Principal-protected assets are what I like to call our "know-so money." It is money we can generally count on receiving throughout our retirement years.

Here is an example of some Red Money assets.

1. Stocks
2. Bonds
3. Mutual funds
4. Brokerage accounts
5. Options
6. Variable annuities

Principal-at-risk assets are assets that do not have a principal-protection feature. These assets are usually in what we think of as the stock market. That could mean the money is invested in stocks that are tracked in a stock market index such as the S&P 500 or the Dow Jones Industrial Average, they could be individual stocks, mutual funds, variable annuities, alternative investments, etc.

Principal-at-risk assets are what I like to call our "hope-so money." It is money that you hope to get a great return on and that you hope won't lose principal.

The real "trick" to designing a successful retirement income plan is having the correct balance between your know-so money and your hope-so money. We will take a closer look at this in a later chapter.

Most of you have probably heard of Warren Buffet. Regardless of what you think of his political views, we can all agree that he seems to know how to make money. Warren Buffet has said that he has two rules that he follows;

Rule No. 1: "Don't Lose Money"

Rule No. 2: "Don't Forget Rule No.1"

It seems that one of the reasons Warren Buffet might have been so successful could be because he understands the power of compound interest. He probably understands that if you lose money in a major downturn in the market, it could take years to make up the loss.

Consider the following question:

If you lose 35 percent of the value of your assets in a market downturn, how much interest do you have to earn to break even?

If you are like most people, you probably answered 35 percent. Many people reason out that they should have to earn back the same percentage they lost to break even.

The following study done by Craig Israelsen, Ph.D., illustrates how devastating a major downturn in the market could be.[2]

Probability of recovery

Loss	Gain needed to re-cover	Chance of recovery from loss within_ years					
		1	2	3	4	5	10
-10%	11.1%	52.5%	74.4%	81.6%	78.4%	77.8%	93.5%
-20%	25%	25.0%	48.7%	68.4%	67.6%	72.2%	93.5%
-35%	54%	0.0%	17.9%	34.2%	56.8%	61.1%	93.5%
-50%	100%	0.0%	0.0%	7.9%	13.5%	36.1%	80.6%
-65%	186%	0.0%	0.0%	0.0%	2.7%	5.6%	61.3%

The S&P 500 is designed to be a leading indicator of U.S. equities and is meant to reflect the risk/return characteristics of the large-cap universe. It is not available for direct investment.

So, the actual interest you would have to earn to break even is 54 percent! This confuses many people, but consider that after the loss there is 35 percent less money to earn interest on. Therefore, you have to earn significantly more than you lost to get back to where you started.

To me, the real alarming statistic here is the probability of re-covery in the number of years it takes to break even. In Dr. Is-realsen's example, if your investments lost 35 percent, the probability of the account being back to even in 10 years is only 93.5 percent for the time period studied!

---

[2] Craig L. Israelsen. 2009. "The Math of Gains and Losses."

If you are in the Retirement Danger Zone — which, if you remember, I said is 10 years prior to retirement and 10 years into retirement — and this happens, it could be devastating to your portfolio. Just imagine you are in the last 10 years of employment before you plan to retire and this happens. It could mean postponing your retirement while trying to earn back the loss. If it happens in the first 10 years into retirement, especially if you are taking income from the portfolio, it could change everything. It might even *cook the goose*. In other words, you might find yourself in a situation where your retirement account has been depleted and cannot provide the income you need or planned for. I'm sure you have seen many people well into their retirement years working at places such as the grocery store, golf course, hardware store, etc. It is quite possible they found themselves in the situations I have previously described. Their goose can no longer produce the golden eggs they need. It is one thing to work because you want to and quite another because you have to, especially when you are in your retirement years.

Dr. Isrealsen's study is a great illustration of why you might want to have goose insurance in the portfolio to help protect against this.

CHAPTER 6

Retirement Paycheck #1: Social Security

Typically, the two largest paychecks you will receive in retirement are your Social Security check and your *pension check*, or, if you didn't have a pension at work, the check you create from retirement assets such as a 401(k), 403(b) or other retirement assets, or in some cases a combination of all three. As you can imagine, it is important to do everything you can to make the most of each one of these sources of retirement income.

Let's take a closer look at check No. 1, Social Security.

Since Social Security can be such a large portion of a retiree's income, it is very important that you understand how it works and how to maximize this paycheck.

Let me give you a little history lesson. The Social Security bill was signed into law by President Franklin Delano Roosevelt on Aug. 14, 1935.

The first payment was made to Ernest Ackerman as a lump sum in January of 1937, for the whopping amount of 17 cents. Since then, over $7.4 TRILLION has been paid out in benefits.

The first monthly payment was made to Ida May Fuller in January 1940. The monthly amount of her first check was $22.54. Her story is really quite a success story as far as a return on her investment is concerned. Ida May Fuller only worked under the Social Security system for three years and paid a total of $24.75 into the system. She retired at age 65 and lived to be 100, which was very unusual for that time period. By age 100, she had collected $22,888.92 from the Social Security system. Not a bad return on an investment of $24.75!

Currently, in order to qualify for Social Security benefits, you must have 40 credits, or about 10 years of work history, to receive benefits.

As we have seen, the Social Security system has been going through a major transformation and upheaval in the past few years. COLAs (cost-of-living adjustments) have been slashed, the full retirement age has been increased, some spousal planning strategies have been eliminated and many more changes are coming that will affect most future recipients.

These changes are being made as part of a plan to hopefully save the Social Security system. The plan is in place for a good reason, because the Social Security paycheck can actually account for more than 60 percent of a person's income in retirement. With deferred credits and COLAs, Social Security might be the only guaranteed stream of income for many people. Yet, statistics show "less than 22 percent of financial professionals fully understand how to maximize lifetime benefits."[3]

While it may seem logical, then, to call up the Social Security Administration for advice on your benefits, think twice. Basically all the Social Security Administration workers are allowed to do is "provide enough information so that claimants can make informed choices, but do not give advice."[4]

Why are they not allowed to give advice? Because they do not have the information to see your complete financial picture, nor are they financial advisors.

Why does that matter? For starters, people expect to receive help and advice from somewhere. In fact, according to one survey, "77 percent of [the respondents to the survey] would expect to receive advice from a Social Security representative ... on how to maximize their Social Security benefits."[5]

I have had several of my clients go into the Social Security office to sign up for their benefits and be given information that was just not correct. For one couple, they visited the Social Security office when it was still possible to use something called a "file and suspend" strategy, which would have greatly benefitted them (this strategy is one of the spousal strategies that is no longer an option, but at the time it was fairly popular). Instead, they were told by a Social Security representative that they could not use this particular strategy. They had previously been to one of my Social Security and Income Planning workshops and knew that what they

---

[3] "Financial Advisors' Role in Influencing Social Security Claiming." Financial Literacy. November 2011. WR-894-SSA, 4-77.

[4] Social Security Administration. 2017. Program Operations Manual System. "GN 00203.004 Taking the Claim." https://secure.ssa.gov/poms.nsf/lnx/0200203004.

[5] Joe Elsasser. LifeHealthPro. Oct. 12, 2011. "Social Security Planning: A New Angle for Your Senior Clients." http://www.lifehealthpro.com/2011/10/12/social-security-planning-a-new-angle-for-your-seni?slreturn=1483730911.

were being told at the Social Security office was not correct. When that happens, we help our clients find and print out the exact language from the Social Security "POMS" manual and have them take the language back to the Social Security office. That usually remedies the situation, as it did for this couple. It is always better to go to the Social Security Administration with instructions rather than questions.

We have also had several clients over the years who were underpaid by Social Security. One client was underpaid due to her having a disabled child who she was the legal guardian of, and the adult child was in her care.

While her circumstances should have qualified her for full Social Security benefits at age 60, the Social Security office was giving her discounted benefits based on her attained age of 62. It is not the job of the Social Security Administration to review your entire circumstances and financial picture and then make recommendations. In this case, once I saw this woman in my office, I realized what happened and was able to provide her with the correct information to take to the Social Security office to have this fixed. She not only got a significant increase in her monthly benefit, she also received a large lump-sum check for the back payments due to her.

This is an area where many people do not plan and, instead of seeking the advice of a qualified financial advisor who can review their financial picture in its entirety, they get their advice from their brother-in-law or the guy who lives next door. Remember, this could be a large percentage of your retirement income and it is vital to get it right.

There has been a lot of talk lately about Social Security going broke in the year 2033. Of course, that is very scary to most of my clients. What would actually happen on the current path we're on is that, if no reforms were put into action, the Social Security trust fund would only be able to pay approximately 75 percent of current benefits by the year 2033. BUT. Reforms have been put in place to help alleviate this, and many more are being discussed and bantered around. It is indeed a point of concern and one that we should push our elected officials to address promptly and correctly. Of course, we know that is a book all in itself! I draw my own conclusions from the fact that most financial professionals believe Social Security will survive, mainly due to the fact that politicians can't afford ticking off the largest voting bloc.[6]

With all that in mind, let's take a look at some of the particulars of this paycheck. As of right now, Social Security is still:

Guaranteed

Inflation-adjusted

Tax-preferred

Provides lifetime income

Let's take a closer look at each one of these benefits.

Guaranteed:

On March 2, 1999, the House of Representatives passed House Joint Resolution 32, which "protects guaranteed lifetime benefits for current retirees and those nearing retirement." H.J.Res. 32, the Social Security Guarantee Initiative, passed by a vote of 416 to 1.

"The resolution expresses the sense of the Congress that the president and the Congress should join in undertaking the Social Security Guarantee Initiative. This initiative would strengthen the

---

[6] Social Security and Medicare Boards of Trustees. Social Security Administration. 2016. "Status of the Social Security and Medicare Programs: A Summary of the 2016 Annual Reports." https://www.ssa.gov/oact/trsum/. Accessed Jan. 6, 2017.

Social Security program and protect the retirement income security of all Americans for the 21st century."[7]

But let's face it, we are dealing with the federal government and, if we can count on one thing, THINGS CHANGE! But for right now, Social Security is guaranteed to be there when we need it, at least for the baby boomer generation.

Inflation-Protected:

3.7%

Average COLA since 1977

The first COLA, or cost-of-living adjustment, was started in 1975 and has averaged around a 3.6 percent increase per year since then.

There has been a COLA every year since, except for 2010, 2011 and 2016 when the COLA was 0 percent. The COLA for 2019 is 2.8 percent. A reduction or elimination of the COLA saves money and increases the Social Security trust fund, but can also be detrimental to people who are starting their Social Security benefits because of increases to Medicare premiums. So there is a fine line between cutting costs and cutting benefits. It might be wise when planning your retirement income to plan on little or no COLAs for Social Security, at least in the near future.[8]

[7] Social Security Legislative Bulletin. Social Security Administration. March 3, 1999. "House Passes House Joint Resolution 32, The Social Security Guarantee Initiative." https://www.ssa.gov/legislation/legis_bulletin_030399.html. Accessed Jan. 6, 2017.
[8] Social Security Administration. 2019. "Cost-of-Living Adjustment (COLA) Information for 2019." https://www.ssa.gov/cola/.

Cost-of-Living Adjustments to Social Security							
Year	COLA	Year	COLA	Year	COLA	Year	COLA
1977	6.4	1988	4.2	1999	1.3	2010	0.0
1978	5.9	1989	4.0	2000	2.5	2011	0.0
1979	6.5	1990	4.7	2001	3.5	2012	3.6
1980	9.9	1991	5.4	2002	2.6	2013	1.7
1981	14.3	1992	3.7	2003	1.4	2014	1.5
1982	11.2	1993	3.0	2004	2.1	2015	1.7
1983	7.4	1994	2.6	2005	2.7	2016	0.0
1984	3.5	1995	2.8	2006	4.1	2017	0.3
1985	3.5	1996	2.6	2007	3.3	2018	2.0
1986	3.1	1997	2.9	2008	2.3	2019	2.8
1987	1.3	1998	2.1	2009	5.8		

Lifetime Income:

As most of you already know, you cannot outlive your Social Security benefits. That really is an amazing benefit, especially if you are one of the fortunate people who live to be 104 and play golf three days a week. Now you have a new reason to stay healthy and active!

Tax-Preferred (but still taxed)

What makes your Social Security income tax-preferred is that the maximum amount of Social Security benefits the government can tax as ordinary income is 85 percent.

This is quite different from the percentage that is taxable from your distributions from a qualified account such as an IRA or 401(k). Where Social Security income is capped at 85 percent, taxable distributions from your qualified retirement accounts are 100 percent taxable.

Let's take a look at Social Security taxation.[9]

---

[9] Social Security Administration. 2017. "Benefits Planner: Income Taxes And Your Social Security Benefits." https://www.ssa.gov/planners/taxes.html. Accessed Jan. 6, 2017.

Tax-Preferred Income		
Total taxable amount if your <u>provisional</u> income is...		
	Single filer	Married filing jointly
0%	< $25,000	< $32,000
50%	$25,000 - $34,000	$32,000 - $44,000
85%	> $34,000	> $44,000

- If you file a "single" tax return and earn less than $25,000, none of your Social Security benefit is taxable.
- If you file a "single" return and earn between $25,000 and $34,000, then 50% of your Social Security benefit is taxable.
- If you are a "single" filer and earn over $34,000, 85% of your Social Security income is subject to taxation.
- If you file a "joint" return and have earnings of less than $32,000, none of your Social Security benefit is taxable.
- If you earn between $32,000 and $44,000, 50% of your benefit is taxable.
- If you earn over $44,000, 85% of your Social Security benefit becomes subject to taxation.

Social Security benefits are taxed using the provisional income formula.

Now, this is different from the adjusted gross income formula that you use for your taxes, where you deduct certain items or expenses from your total income. It is also different from the modified adjusted gross income formula (what a mouthful!).

Instead, the provisional income that your Social Security taxes are based on is:[10]

---

[10] Ibid.

Provisional income = AGI (adjusted gross income) + 1/2 of Social Security benefits + tax-exempt interest

Take note that the formula <u>does include</u> tax-exempt interest. This is a shocker to most people because this would include interest from your tax-free bonds. Only in the world of politicians would a tax-free bond actually cause you to pay more taxes in a formula they created.

PLANNING OPPORTUNITY!

There are several income planning strategies that can be used to potentially reduce provisional income, which in turn can possibly reduce the taxation on Social Security benefits.

Let me show you an example of how a few of these strategies were applied in my office. I have a client who was paying taxes on 85 percent of his Social Security benefits when we first met. After our initial strategy session, I found out that he was paying these taxes unnecessarily.

What caused his tax problem? One of his large, interest-producing assets was included in his provisional income calculation. This interest was income that he did not need and was not using, but he was losing a large portion of it in taxes to his Social Security. We implemented a strategy to take advantage of tax-deferred planning, placing his interest in tax-deferred accounts and reducing the taxation of his Social Security benefits to zero! In his case, all that money he was paying unnecessarily in taxes was now back in his pocket.

What Is FRA and Why Is It So Important?

It is very important to be aware of your FRA, or *full retirement age*. At FRA, you become eligible for full federal benefits, and there is no longer a reduction in your Social Security income for "starting early." In addition to getting your full benefit, you are also allowed to earn as much as you can without the government applying an "earnings test" to your benefits.

Once you know what your FRA is, then you can figure what your PIA, or primary insurance amount is, which is just a fancy way of saying you can figure out what your monthly income will be.

I have included the following chart so you can calculate what your FRA is.[11]

Your Full Retirement Age	
Year of Birth	Full Retirement Age
1937 or earlier	65
1938	65 and 2 months
1939	65 and 4 months
1940	65 and 6 months
1941	65 and 8 months
1942	65 and 10 months
1943—1954	66
1955	66 and 2 months
1956	66 and 4 months
1957	66 and 6 months
1958	66 and 8 months
1959	66 and 10 months
1960 or later	67

The Social Security Administration calculates your monthly income from Social Security using your top 35 earnings years to figure your average indexed monthly earnings (AIME). Then they use a tool called the bend point formula to calculate your benefit amount. This formula and a lot more information can be found on

---

[11] Social Security Administration. 2017. "Retirement Planner: Full Retirement Age." https://www.ssa.gov/planners/retire/retirechart.html. Accessed Jan. 17, 2017.

the Social Security Administration's website at ssa.gov. I strongly suggest that you go on the website and set up your own account. This will allow you to check one very important thing, your earnings history. If you have zeros in your earnings history, they will count them and reduce your monthly income. If you can prove to the Social Security Administration that you had earnings in any of those "zero" years, they will correct your record. This could increase your benefit, so it is very important to look at this. You will also be able to get an estimate on what your benefit will be, based on your current earnings history.

In September 2014, the Social Security Administration began mailing Social Security statements to workers attaining ages 25, 30, 35, 40, 45, 50, 55, 60 and over who aren't receiving Social Security benefits and do not yet have a "My Social Security" account. They mail the statements three months prior to your birthday.

Now that you have at least a basic understanding of how we get to the monthly income amount you can expect to receive at FRA, let's move on to the meat of the Social Security discussion for most of us. That is, how can you make the most of this important monthly benefit?

It starts with what age you claim your benefit. The following chart illustrates the percentage of Social Security income that you surrender by claiming early and the percentage you gain by deferring your benefits.

WHY WOULD **YOU** SURRENDER?

62	63	64	65	FRA	67	68	69	70
-25%	-20%	-13.3%	-6.7%	0	+8%	+16%	+24%	+32%

% of PIA (Primary Insurance Amount)

Source: SSA.gov FRA of 66

If you saved money at your local bank for 30 or 40 years and you went in to the bank to start taking income at age 62 and they told you that you would receive 25 percent less, would you be upset? Of course you would, and that is basically what happens when you start taking your Social Security benefit at age 62.

Can or should everyone wait until full retirement age to start collecting their benefits? Not necessarily. There is a very detailed decision-making process that is involved in determining when to start receiving your benefits.

Some of the factors involved are:

- Personal health issues
- Family health issues
- Longevity
- Income needs
- Planning strategies

It is important to remember that working with a financial advisor to examine these factors collectively can be a great aid. I have a client, James, who made his Social Security claiming decision solely based on his family history. He shared with me that both of his parents passed away in their early- to mid-70s from heart disease. His parents both had very unhealthy habits, including smoking and eating an unhealthy diet. Even though he lived a much healthier lifestyle than his parents did, including not smoking and trying to eat healthier, he was convinced he would experience the same limited longevity as his parents. You might say his perception was shaped more by his parents' experiences than by his own. He made the decision to start drawing his Social Security benefits at age 62 because both of his parents died at a relatively young age. James is now in his late 80s and is still quite healthy. Perhaps he should have reassessed his decision based on current circumstances instead of sticking to reasoning he had so many years prior to him turning 62. That decision was most likely made when the yield sign was yellow instead of red and white, as it currently is. Remember, things change. Has your perspective?

Let's consider the impact on the amount of your Social Security check, based on the number of years you can wait before deciding to start your benefit. Just for example, let's say that your Social Security check, if taken at age 62, would be $1,200. If your full retirement age is 66, then the amount of your check will go up approximately 25 percent, or 6.25 percent each year for four years. We can also add a COLA percentage to this calculation if we want to. Just to be conservative, let's say the COLA averages 1 percent per year, so your check should increase approximately 7.25 percent per year until age 66. So, if you can wait until age 63 to start your benefit, you would receive $1,287 per month. Age 64, $1,380. Age 65, $1,480 and at age 66, $1,587. If you can go beyond your full retirement age of 66, the benefit will increase by 8 percent per year, and as we can see in the following numbers, if you can wait, that is a substantial increase. It works out to $1,713 per month at age 67, $1,850 at age 68, $1,998 at age 69 and $2,157 at age 70. Can everyone wait until age 70 to start their benefit? Probably not, because not everyone is in the same situation in life. But I wanted to illustrate the benefit of waiting if your situation allows you to. By the way, what investment out there right now is paying 6.25 to 8 percent per year, guaranteed?

Another couple I advise made their decision based more on their ability to provide the income needed for their retirement. Their financial situation made it possible for them to defer their Social Security benefits until they reached age 70 so they could maximize their income. The reason they could do this is that they had a 401(k) and other retirement savings to provide them with income, replacing the amount Social Security would have provided them. This couple was already at their full retirement age when they retired and this decision allowed them to let their Social Security benefits continue to grow at 8 percent until age 70, giving them a 32 percent higher payout in monthly income. Longevity was not a big factor in their decision-making process as far as when they would take their Social Security benefits. It was more important to them to receive the significantly higher payout at age 70. By receiving the higher Social Security payout, they needed to use less of their retirement accounts to give them the retirement income they needed.

Who made the right decision? I wouldn't say either one made a wrong decision. Each decision on when to claim Social Security benefits is a very personal one. However, as an advisor, it is my job to help people make the decision that benefits them the most, which might not always match the decisions or perceptions they made years earlier. It is said that hindsight is 20/20, however, perhaps if James viewed his Social Security decision based on facts and numbers and less on emotion he might have made a different choice and be enjoying a much larger Social Security check today.

PLANNING OPPORTUNITY!

This is an area where designing a planning strategy with a qualified financial advisor might be very beneficial. In a situation where you might have other assets that can be used for income in the early years of retirement, you might be able to allow your Social Security benefit to grow to age 70. Each year after FRA, your benefit grows by approximately 8 percent per year. As illustrated before, this can amount to a 32 percent increase in your benefit payment if your FRA is age 66, a 24 percent increase if your FRA is age 67. Also, COLA increases could increase the benefit amount during that time as well.

Taking Social Security Early

We have discussed some advantages of delaying your Social Security benefits. Not only will filing earlier than full retirement age

(FRA) result in a lower monthly check, there is also an "earnings test" for those who decide to start their benefits before FRA.

As of 2017, the earnings test will be applied for any income over $17,640 a year. For every $2 you earn over the $17,640 limit, the Social Security Administration will deduct $1 from your monthly check.

In the year you turn FRA, the limit increases to $46,920 and the deduction is softened a little to $1 for every $3 you earn. This rule usually is a bit confusing to people, partly because, as you may note, it is "in the year you turn FRA," because starting the month you turn FRA, you are no longer subject to the earnings test.[12, 13]

Remember, if you decide to take a job that pays you income over the limit, the amount the Social Security Administration deducts from your benefits isn't truly lost. Your benefit will be recalculated and potentially increased at your full retirement age to account for benefits withheld due to the earnings you received at the point you were earning money while receiving benefits.

Spousal Benefits

A spouse may file for spousal benefits as long as the primary worker has filed for his or her own benefits. If the primary worker files at FRA and their FRA is age 66, the spouse can receive 35 percent of the filers benefit at age 62. If the spouse waits until FRA, they can receive 50 percent of the filers benefit. If the primary worker's FRA is age 67, the benefits change accordingly.

---

[12] Social Security Administration. 2017. "Exempt Amounts Under the Earnings Test." https://www.ssa.gov/oact/cola/rtea.html. Accessed Jan. 6, 2017.

[13] Earnings test numbers are current for 2017, and are updated every year on ssa.gov.

What Will Your Spouse Get?		
Age	FRA 66	FRA 67
62	35.0%	32.5%
63	37.5%	35.0%
64	41.7%	37.5%
65	45.8%	41.7%
66	50.0%	45.8%
67	50.0%	50.0%

Ex-spouse benefits

There are ex-spouse benefits as long as the following criteria have been met.

The marriage must have lasted 10 years.

You must have been divorced for at least 2 years.

The claimer must be unmarried.

What happens if a spouse dies?

The living spouse or divorced living spouse can step into the greater of the 2 individual benefits.

The spouse can elect as early as age 60 with reduced benefits. They can also remarry after age 60 and still collect their deceased former spouse's benefits.

Now, that's a lot of fast facts, I know, but they play out in different ways depending on everyone's personal scenarios.

Let's look at a case study:

Ron – 57   Betty – 59 ½

Ron and Betty have been dating for years. Betty is a widow whose husband died at the age of 61 before receiving Social Security benefits. Ron and Betty are planning on going to Vegas to get re-married next weekend.

Q: Is Betty currently eligible for her widow's benefit?

A: No. ... Betty is not disabled and she is not 60.

Q: How could the marriage affect Betty's eligibility?

A: If she re-marries before the age of 60, she will lose access to her widow's benefit.

As you can see, the decision of when to take your Social Security benefits is a decision that needs very careful consideration. Some decisions, if made incorrectly, could cost literally thousands of dollars in lost benefits over the years.

This is a great place to stress the importance of working with a financial advisor who can not only show you different claiming strategies, but who can outline tax consequences and ways that your Social Security benefits will work with your other assets to maximize your retirement income. There are several more claiming strategies that have not been discussed here that should be considered on a case-by-case basis. Hopefully, this example gives you a solid idea of how important it is to consider your options when deciding to claim your Social Security benefits and why you should work with a financial advisor that has the knowledge to guide you through these major decisions of life.

I mentioned earlier that some are concerned about the future viability of Social Security and if its trust fund will continue to pay out after 2033. Currently, there are many reforms being suggested and implemented to fix the issues with Social Security. Many have already been instituted and many are slated for future implementation.

Some of the reforms are:[14]

 Increase maximum earnings subject to the Social Security tax.

 Raise the full retirement age (FRA).

---

[14] Emily Brandon. Money, US News. April 25, 2016. "6 Ways to Fix Social Security's Finances." http://money.usnews.com/money/blogs/planning-to-retire/articles/2016-04-15/6-ways-to-fix-social-securitys-finances. Accessed Jan. 6, 2017.

 Raise the early retirement age and/or increase the penalty for taking benefits early.

 Lower primary insurance amounts (PIA) for future retirees.

 Reduce cost-of-living adjustments (COLA).

A primary example of these reforms being instituted are the removal or modification of some key strategies under the "Tax Cuts and Jobs Act of 2019."

For example:

The File and Suspend strategy.

Previously, if you reached your full retirement age you could file for your Social Security benefits and then immediately suspend the benefit payment and allow your benefit amount to continue to grow. At the same time, your spouse could file for spousal benefits, as long as they are at least age 62, while your benefit would be growing at approximately 8% until you start payments or reach age 70. Then, if your spouse is accumulating their own benefit and if it is higher, they can switch to their own benefit. Sounds like a great strategy, right?

Now this strategy has been limited to only a certain bracket of people. The new rule says that If you were born on 04/30/1950 or earlier and attained FRA by 04/29/2016 you were eligible. It is still available but to a much smaller group.

Do you have a GAME PLAN for Social Security?

QUIZ TIME!

Please take the time to take the Social Security quiz. It is included to help you see what you have retained, or what you might need to go back and review about Social Security.

1. Social Security could account for more than____% of a person's income in retirement.
2. What are the 4 major benefits to Social Security?
    1.
    2.
    3.
    4.
3. The maximum amount of Social Security that can be taxed as ordinary income is _____%.
4. What are FRA and PIA? _____and_____
5. What is your FRA if you were born in 1950? _____
6. If your FRA is age 66, and you have filed for benefits and your spouse is age 64 and files under your work record, what percentage of your benefit will they receive? _____%.

Answers on page 113.

CHAPTER 7

Retirement Paycheck #2: Retirement Assets

AND HOW TO NAVIGATE THE RETIREMENT
DANGER ZONE

L et's assume you are now in the Retirement Danger Zone, 10 years before and 10 years after your retirement date. This is where you don't want to cook the goose! Now is the time to really protect that retirement nest egg, which hopefully will produce those golden eggs of retirement income for you.

Do you have a game plan for retirement? Do you have strategies to hopefully provide you with the income you need to live the retirement you have always dreamed of? By now you know that it is folly to enter retirement without a well-thought-out plan. Sticking your head in the sand and hoping for the best rarely works out like we hope it will. In order to make a wise plan it is important to understand the landscape, or phases of retirement.

Let's take a closer, more in-depth look at two critical phases of retirement, the *accumulation* phase and the *distribution and protection* phase.

RETIREMENT **DANGER ZONE**

ACCUMULATION	DISTRIBUTION & PROTECTION
ROI = Return on Investment	ROI = Reliability of Income

29,029 ft.

DANGER ZONE

26,000 ft.

Do you recognize this mountain? You are correct if you think it is Mount Everest. Everest is 29,029 feet high and there is an actual "death zone" at 26,000 feet. This is where the risks of climbing the mountain are the greatest and where the majority of deaths occur. I can't believe people actually want to climb this mountain!

Approximately 15 years ago, I was sitting in an audience listening to Jon Krakauer, a man who climbed Mount Everest and lived to tell about it. Everyone in the audience was on the edge of their seats as he explained the climb in great, heart-breaking detail, including how several of his climbing companions lost their lives. The speaker had to stop several times and choke back the tears as he told about his friends, their lives and the families they left behind. He explained that his friends perished in the death zone of Mount Everest. Fatalities were both on the way up in the death zone and on the way down.

The reasons they did not make it included not following the rules, poor planning and unforeseen issues that caused them to not be able to finish, like sickness and just plain running out of energy to complete the task.

As I sat there, I began to think about how that applies to so many decisions, or lack of decision-making, in our lives. I also began to apply it to people I had seen in my office or even the situation with my father, making such an uninformed, bad decision that had severe consequences for my mother. I decided the concept of the death zone on Mount Everest could be applied in other areas of our lives, especially to the area of planning for financial peace in retirement.

I have changed the death zone for my income planning purposes to the Retirement Danger Zone in my "Don't Cook the Goose Retirement Income Planning" process. The danger zone is the last 10 years before retirement and the first 10 years into retirement. This is a critical period of time when a sharp decline in the stock market could be detrimental to the retirement plan, especially if the assets are in a position that is too risky.

In my analogy to Mount Everest, I look at the accumulation phase of our investing life as climbing up the mountain, or growing our nest egg or our Golden Goose. During these years we are looking for ROI, or return on investment. These are the years, especially when we are younger, when we are focused primarily on growth, because we have time to potentially make up any losses that may occur in our investments. Therefore, many people are invested in areas with more risk to try to get a better return.

Once we have reached retirement at the top and start down the mountain, we enter into the distribution phase, or as I like to say, the distribution and *protection* phase of retirement.

We are still looking for ROI at that time, but the meaning of ROI then changes from return on investment to reliability of income. We are trying to build reliable sources of income that might

Unique Risks Facing Those in the Retirement Danger Zone:
Longevity
Health
Inflation
Sequence of Returns
Market Volatility
Legacy Plans

Focus: Reliability of Income

have to last 30 years or more into retirement. This is when you want to protect the goose — your retirement account — that will be responsible for your retirement income. You need to build monthly income you can count on to be there regardless of how long you live.

During the distribution and protection phase, we all face some very unique risks. These are risks we must consider when putting together a well-thought-out plan for our retirement years.

One risk is longevity. As we discussed, there is no doubt that people are living longer. Protecting our portfolios becomes extremely important to help insure that our incomes will last as long as we need. This is where I suggest you be very conservative in any projections of future returns. I have seen too many people in my office who planned their retirement on a projected growth that was just way too high for these times of low interest rates. Therefore, they were in trouble because the actual growth of their accounts did not measure up to the projected growth, and their retirement accounts were running out of money. In other words, their *goose was nearly cooked.*

Health risk is one we can all relate to. I'm sure everyone reading this has either had a friend or someone in their family who has had a health issue that threatened their retirement savings in one way or another. Typically this happens when people are underinsured for health insurance or even long-term-care needs. I have actually seen people decide to retire without even considering what they will do for health insurance. This is a big part of your pre-retirement planning, especially if you are retiring prior to age 65. To consider entering into retirement without health insurance that allows you to accurately calculate your risk is absolute folly. Let me give you a true story of what could possibly happen without the proper health insurance coverage — in this case, no health insurance coverage.

Ken and Mary decided to semi-retire, without health insurance of any kind, against the advice of their advisor. Ken was 61 and Mary was 60. They had the unshakeable philosophy that they would be fine without health insurance until they reached 65, when they could qualify for Medicare. They seemed to be quite healthy and had big plans for their future. They owned their home and had a small at-home business that was quite successful at supplementing their retirement income needs. At age 63, Ken had a massive heart attack and had to be flown to an out-of-state hospital to save his life. He was in the hospital for 38 days, then in a rehabilitation facility for months after his discharge from the hospital. He never fully recovered and passed away before turning 65. However, Mary was not able to pay the astronomical medical bills. After their retirement accounts were drained down and their home business sold, Mary had to apply for Medicaid benefits to help pay the remaining balances. They were devastated in many ways, including financially. Mary was left with no retirement income other than her husband's Social Security income, no home business and a mortgage on her house. Mary's life drastically changed.

Please make sure you have health insurance coverage as a part of your retirement planning. If you are eligible for Medicare parts A and B, it is wise to research and consider a Medicare supplement plan, as well, to give you more complete coverage.

Another obvious risk is inflation. Inflation seems to be one of those things you can count on to always go up, at least in the last few decades. Inflation can be very detrimental to a retirement account if you lack proper planning. To imagine how inflation could potentially destroy your retirement plan, just stop and think what you paid for a house, car, gas or groceries just 20 years ago. Do you still remember when you could buy a candy bar for a nickel? How about when you could fill your car up on less than $10? Or do you remember the McDonald's slogan that you could eat there for a dollar and still get change back? Many people I see are paying more for their property taxes each year than they did for their first mortgage. Remember, your retirement could be as long as 30 or 40 years. Do you think prices will go up over that many years?

Inflation is very real and can chip away at your purchasing power. Make sure inflation protection is part of your plan when you are considering whether to retire.

There are some very real risks in the Retirement Danger Zone. Two of the more dangerous risks we face are the risk of market volatility and a bad sequence of returns, especially when distributions are being taken from the portfolio. Let's take a look at some examples.

Let's go back 30 years and invest $500,000 in the S&P 500 and see what it would have done. For this example, the years I used were from 1979 to 2009.

30-year market performance

	Beginning	S&P return	End of year
1	$500,000	28%	$640,000
2	$640,000	-10%	$576,000
3	$576,000	15%	$662,400
4	$662,400	17%	$775,008
5	$775,008	1%	$782,758
6	$782,758	26%	$986,275
7	$986,275	15%	$1,134,216
8	$1,134,216	2%	$1,156,901
9	$1,156,901	12%	$1,295,729
10	$1,295,729	27%	$1,645,576
11	$1,645,576	-7%	$1,530,385
12	$1,530,385	26%	$1,928,286
13	$1,928,286	5%	$2,024,700
14	$2,024,700	7%	$2,166,429
15	$2,166,429	-2%	$2,123,100
16	$2,123,100	34%	$2,844,954
17	$2,844,954	20%	$3,413,945
18	$3,413,945	31%	$4,472,268
19	$4,472,268	27%	$5,679,781
20	$5,679,781	20%	$6,815,737
21	$6,815,737	-10%	$6,134,163
22	$6,134,163	-13%	$5,336,722
23	$5,336,722	-23%	$4,109,276
24	$4,109,276	26%	$5,177,688
25	$5,177,688	9%	$5,643,680
26	$5,643,680	3%	$5,812,990
27	$5,812,990	14%	$6,626,808
28	$6,626,808	4%	$6,891,881
29	$6,891,881	-38%	$4,272,966
30	$4,272,966	20%	$5,127,559

In this sequence of returns, 30 years later the account would have been worth more than $5 million.

Now let's start taking $30,000 a year from the account, plus 3 percent to account for an average annual inflation of 3 percent over the same time period. You will notice, in the last 10 years, there was a bad sequence of returns. These included the years of 2000 to 2002 and 2008, where the stock market had significant losses. In this scenario, you can see those years of market turbulence with income withdrawals were detrimental to the portfolio, but they were at the end of the 30-year period, so there was still a pretty nice balance in the account.

Withdrawals during a 30-year span
Withdrawals include a 3% annual step to account for infla-
tion

	Beginning	S&P return	Withdrawal	End of year
1	$500,000	28%	$30,000	$610,000
2	$610,000	-10%	$30,900	$518,100
3	$518,100	15%	$31,827	$563,988
4	$563,988	17%	$32,782	$627,084
5	$627,084	1%	$33,765	$599,590
6	$599,590	26%	$34,778	$720,705
7	$720,705	15%	$35,822	$792,989
8	$792,989	2%	$36,896	$771,953
9	$771,953	12%	$38,003	$826,584
10	$826,584	27%	$39,143	$1,010,618
11	$1,010,618	-7%	$40,317	$899,557
12	$899,557	26%	$41,527	$1,091,915
13	$1,091,915	5%	$42,773	$1,103,738
14	$1,103,738	7%	$44,056	$1,136,944
15	$1,136,944	-2%	$45,378	$1,068,827
16	$1,068,827	34%	$46,739	$1,385,490
17	$1,385,490	20%	$48,141	$1,614,446
18	$1,614,446	31%	$49,585	$2,065,339
19	$2,065,339	27%	$51,073	$2,571,908
20	$2,571,908	20%	$52,605	$3,033,684
21	$3,033,684	-10%	$54,183	$2,676,133
22	$2,676,133	-13%	$55,809	$2,272,427
23	$2,272,427	-23%	$57,483	$1,692,285
24	$1,692,285	26%	$59,208	$2,073,072
25	$2,073,072	9%	$60,984	$2,198,665
26	$2,198,665	3%	$62,813	$2,201,811
27	$2,201,811	14%	$64,698	$2,445,367
28	$2,445,367	4%	$66,639	$2,476,543
29	$2,476,543	-38%	$68,638	$1,466,819
30	$1,466,819	20%	$70,697	$1,689,486

Now, let's flip this scenario over and start the withdrawals with the bad sequence of returns in the first 10 years of retirement.

Withdrawals during a 30-year span, REVERSED
Withdrawals include a 3% annual step to account for inflation

	Beginning	S&P REVERSE	RE-	Withdrawal	Ending Value
1	$500,000	20%		$30,000	$570,000
2	$570,000	-38%		$30,900	$322,500
3	$322,500	4%		$31,827	$303,573
4	$303,573	14%		$32,782	$313,291
5	$313,291	3%		$33,765	$288,925
6	$288,925	9%		$34,778	$280,150
7	$280,150	26%		$35,822	$317,167
8	$317,167	-23%		$36,896	$207,323
9	$207,323	-13%		$38,003	$142,368
10	$142,368	-10%		$39,143	$88,988
11	$88,988	20%		$40,317	$66,468
12	$66,468	27%		$41,527	$42,887
13	$42,887	31%		$42,773	$13,409
14	$13,409	20%		$44,056	-$27,965

What happened? This person was out of money in 14 years! They cooked the goose!

This is a real world example of how a bad sequence of returns in the Retirement Danger Zone can be totally devastating if there is not enough protection, or goose insurance, in the portfolio.

Over the 30-plus years I have been in the financial services business, I have consulted with hundreds of clients, and one of the first things I do is assess how their investments are currently allocated. The majority of the time, I find that what they think or what they want and what is reality are two vastly different things. Most people have no idea how aggressive their portfolios are until we have a sharp downturn in the market and it is too late. The realization comes when they get their statement and they have lost a substantial amount of their retirement dollars.

Most of the time, this is attributed to a lack of access to a financial professional whom they can trust to give them good advice. Some people are "self-managing" their 401(k) accounts at work or their IRAs once they retire, and that is most likely not their area of expertise. Many of those self-managers obtain their investment advice from their neighbor, co-worker or a family member. Often, I find those who love to tell you how great they are doing managing their own accounts usually tell you only about the gains and not the losses they have incurred. It is like the chronic gambler who brags about their winnings without admitting their losses, which in many cases are significantly larger.

The following pie chart on the left is typical of the portfolio allocation that I see when most people come in for their first appointment and the one on the right is where they thought they were and where they actually wanted to be. How does this happen to them? Why is the picture of what they wanted their portfolio to look like and what it actually looks like so drastically different? I think there are several reasons, but two are the most common ones I see.

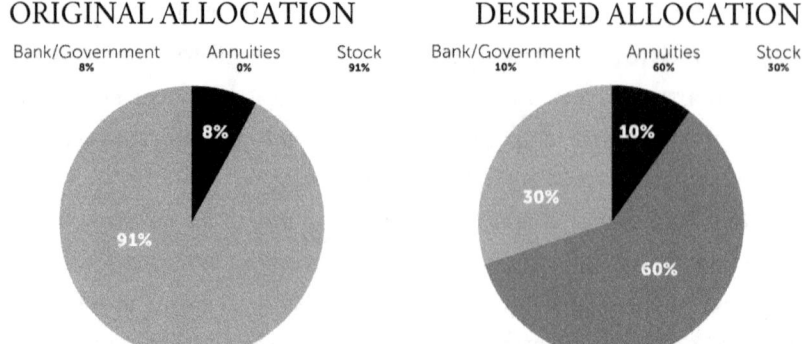

ORIGINAL ALLOCATION

| Bank/Government | Annuities | Stock |
| 8% | 0% | 91% |

DESIRED ALLOCATION

| Bank/Government | Annuities | Stock |
| 10% | 60% | 30% |

The first reason could be that they were "sold" a product without the salesperson doing much — if any — due-diligence into what their risk tolerance was or what their retirement goals even looked like. The product could have been sold many years previously, when the person was in a totally different age bracket, with totally different circumstances. Then, the salesperson may never have followed up on the situation because of negligence, or lack of expertise, or because he or she was no longer working in the industry (this last scenario is very common due to the extremely high employee turnover in the financial services industry).

The second reason is that a lot of people are self-managing their investment portfolios. I am not saying that people can't do this successfully, because I have met people who have done it very successfully. However, the majority of people do not have the time, patience or expertise to make all of these decisions on their own. Another phenomenon I have witnessed in my office with self-managers is that many times the husband and wife are not on the same page, and that is a constant source of friction in their household. I once had a physician in one of my classes who raised his hand as I was discussing self-managers. He told the class that he was one of the self-managers I was describing.

"I think I am a pretty good physician but as far as an investment manager, not so good. I invested $10,000 for my son when he was born. Today, my son is nearly 22 years old and his account is worth just under the $10,000 I originally started with." He went on to say, "My wife told me to stick to practicing medicine and get a good financial advisor to invest the money, I should have listened to her."

To which his wife loudly responded, "Amen!"

It is my experience that life goes much smoother when the couples agree on the plan together.

As you can imagine, the failure rate of people who try to make money by trading stocks themselves is very high! I am not saying this just so you will go to a financial advisor for help; it is just what I have observed in my practice. What is the standard rule of investing? Buy low, sell high, right? What usually happens is just the opposite of what is supposed to happen.

Think about this for a minute, when do you hear about a great investment or the latest hot stock? When it is just starting out? Or rather when it is already soaring and the price is high? We almost always hear about it when all the excitement is happening. The stock is in the news, your friends are telling you how great it is and how much money they have made! So you buy some, and then what happens? That's right, the run is over and the stock price starts going the other way and the majority of people will panic and sell when the stock bottoms out. Ironically, this is what most people do, it is just human nature.

If this happens to someone who is trying to self-manage their investments, often they will get discouraged and abandon the idea and not re-visit the portfolio in fear of making another mistake. This can lead to the asset mix being too skewed in one direction, and the returns could be negatively affected or worse. In some circumstances, the principal could be greatly depleted, which again is another way of saying *the goose is cooked*.

We protect everything with insurance, don't we? Car, house, boat, motorcycle, mortgage, our health, our lives! Shouldn't we be

putting insurance on the thing that funds all this? OUR RETIRE-
MENT INCOME? OUR NEST EGG? OUR GOLDEN GOOSE?

The next two charts illustrate the benefit of putting some goose
insurance, or some safer assets, in the portfolio. The first chart is
an example of a portfolio that is heavily weighted in stocks that
the S&P 500 comprises during the years of 2000 to 2009. The
overall return for the portfolio over that time period was a NEG-
ATIVE 19 percent. This was without taking any distributions. I
purposefully used the years of 2000 to 2009, to illustrate years
when the market had a bad sequence of returns.

10-Year Performance of Original Allocations

	S&P 500	Bank/ Gov.	Annui- ties	Stock	Total	$ Gain/ Loss	% Gain/ Loss
		$50,000	$0	$510,000	$560,000		
2000	-11.81%	$50,500	$0	$449,769	$500,269	-$59,731	-11%
2001	-10.02%	$51,005	$0	$404,702	$455,707	-$44,562	-9%
2002	-21.27%	$51,515	$0	$318,622	$370,137	-$85,570	-19%
2003	21.94%	$52,030	$0	$388,528	$440,558	$70,421	19%
2004	8.44%	$52,551	$0	$421,319	$473,870	$33,312	8%
2005	5.55%	$53,076	$0	$444,703	$497,779	$23,909	5%
2006	11.64%	$53,607	$0	$496,466	$550,073	$52,294	11%
2007	2.15%	$54,143	$0	$507,140	$561,283	$11,210	2%
2008	-35.61%	$54,684	$0	$326,547	$381,232	-$180,051	-32%
2009	21.59%	$55,231	$0	$397,049	$452,280	$71,048	19%
	Total	$55,231	$0	$397,049	$452,280	-$107,720	-19%

*This chart is provided for informational purposes only and is not a
solicitation or recommendation of any investment strategy. Investments
and/or investment strategies involve risk, including the possible loss of
principal. There is no assurance that any investment strategy will achieve
its objectives.*

The second chart shows the same period of time, but with a more conservative portfolio mix. In this particular case, we used a fixed index annuity, which provides protection of the principal, based on the claims-paying ability of an insurance company, should the market decline. The end result, in the same period of time, was a POSITIVE 12 percent. Adding more bonds to the mix can potentially have a similar effect on the portfolio.

By protecting the downside, we potentially have more money to grow when the market is doing better.

10-Year Performance of Desired Allocations

	S&P 500	Bank/ Gov.	Annui-ties	Stock	Total	$ Gain/ Loss	% Gain/ Loss
			$50,000	$336,000	$168,000	$554,000	
2000	-11.81%	$50,500	$336,000	$148,159	$534,659	-$19,341	-3%
2001	-10.02%	$51,005	$336,000	$133,314	$520,319	-$14,341	-3%
2002	-21.27%	$51,515	$336,000	$104,958	$492,473	-$27,846	-5%
2003	21.94%	$52,030	$352,800	$127,986	$532,816	$40,343	8%
2004	8.44%	$52,551	$370,440	$138,788	$561,778	$28,962	5%
2005	5.55%	$53,076	$388,962	$146,490	$588,528	$26,750	5%
2006	11.64%	$53,607	$408,410	$163,542	$625,559	$37,030	6%
2007	2.15%	$54,143	$417,191	$167,058	$638,392	$12,833	2%
2008	-35.61%	$54,684	$417,191	$107,569	$579,444	-$58,948	-9%
2009	21.59%	$55,231	$438,051	$130,793	$624,074	$44,630	8%
	Total	$55,231	$438,051	$130,793	$624,074	$70,074	12%

This chart is provided for informational purposes only and is not a solicitation or recommendation of any investment strategy. Investments and/or investment strategies involve risk, including the possible loss of principal. There is no assurance that any investment strategy will achieve its objectives.

10-Year Performance
Original vs. Desired Allocations

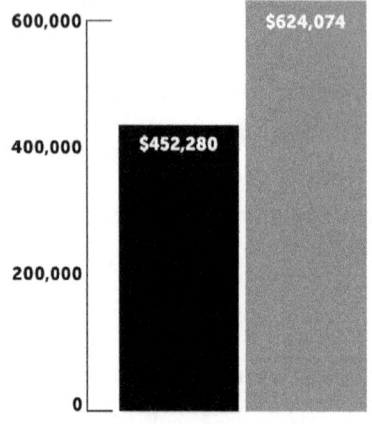

Remember the two rules in a previous chapter of a rather successful investor: "Rule No. 1, Don't Lose Money and Rule No. 2, Don't Forget Rule No. 1." This is a great example of why those are important rules, especially since we do not know when there will be a bad sequence of returns.

Why do we need to add goose insurance to our portfolios when we are in or approaching the Retirement Danger Zone? Remember our chart by Craig Israelsen, Ph.D.? In his example, if the portfolio lost 35 percent, you would have to earn 54 percent to break even, and you might have to wait 10 years or more for this to happen. Let's assume you wanted to retire at age 62, but in the 10 years prior to you turning age 62, the market plummeted as it did in 2001, 2002 and 2008. How would that impact your desire to retire at age 62? The impact most likely would have been devastating, leaving you with choices that were not what you planned. You might have to make choices such as working additional years to hopefully make up for the losses in your retirement accounts or retiring on significantly less income that you had hoped or planned for.

PLANNING OPPORTUNITY!

If you are in or close to that Retirement Danger Zone — 10 years prior to when you would like to retire and the first 10 years into retirement — make sure you have a portfolio review done immediately by a competent financial advisor to see if your investments are allocated correctly and will meet your goals to protect the goose laying your golden retirement eggs.

An important part of your review should be a personal risk profile questionnaire to make sure your investments match up to your risk tolerance.

CHAPTER 8

Maximize Your Income

I t is your job as an investor to make sure you are maximizing every source of income that you have, wouldn't you agree? That is also the job of a good financial advisor. Make sure you specifically tell the financial advisor you choose to work with what your specific goals and desires are to successfully take you through your retirement years.

Many times, accomplishing your goals can be a matter of timing. For example, when do you start Social Security? Can you afford to let your benefit grow until FRA or perhaps even age 70? Are you going to work during retirement and can you hold off on turning the income on from the 401(k)? Do you have a pension that you have to take, allowing you to let another source of income grow for a period of time? What are your income taxes going to be? What strategies can you use to reduce those income taxes, giving you more money to live on throughout your retirement years? There are many strategies you can use to help maximize all your sources of income, and of course it is important to do just that. I can't emphasize enough that this is a decision that can affect your life for 30 years or more; it's important to take the time to make the best decisions possible.

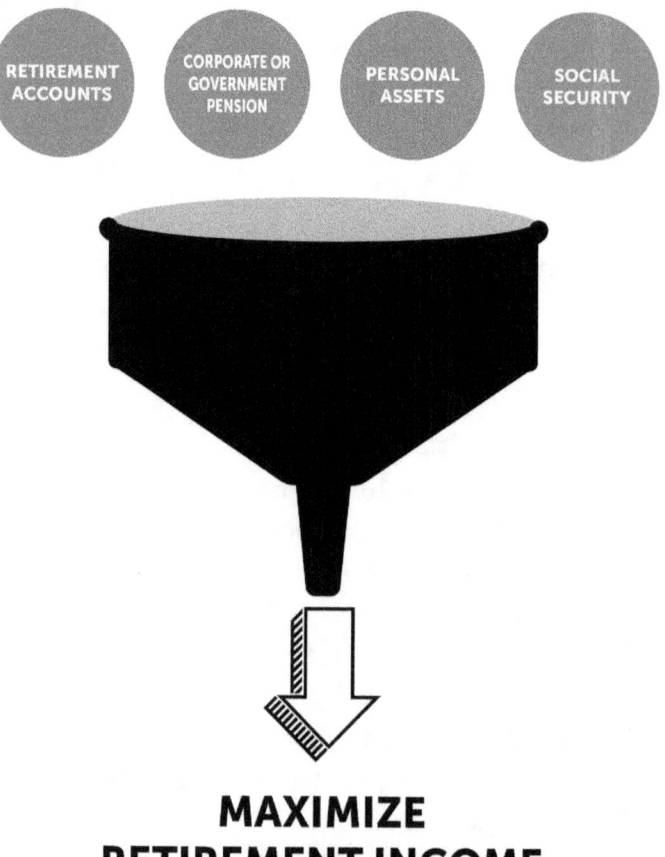

MAXIMIZE
RETIREMENT INCOME

If you are going to work with a financial advisor, make sure it is someone who is really listening to your goals and dreams for retirement. Be prepared for a realistic picture of what your retirement income will look like. Don't fall for the pie-in-the-sky projected returns. Plan for worst-case scenarios and see if your retirement plan will still work. In other words, put your portfolio through a mock "stress test" to see if it can handle the tough times. If your advisor has the right tools, he or she can put together many scenarios, illustrating your different sources of income and how they can work together to maximize each other.

As part of my initial consultation with new clients, I always put their existing investments through this stress test, comparing their current holdings to several different periods in history where the stock market has had a serious decline to see how their portfolios would have been impacted. The stress test looks at several different periods of turmoil in the market, such as the years of 2000 to 2002, and 2008, where the stock market had severe losses. I also look at the periods of time when the market had positive returns to see how much the portfolio would have grown during those times. We can then construct a portfolio of investments based on several different factors, including how much risk the client does or does not want to take. After we've tweaked investments, we can then run the new portfolio mix through the stress test to see how it would have stood up to major downturns in the past and have a clearer picture of what might happen in the future.

To show you how this plays out in reality, let me tell you about a recent client I worked with, I will call him Bruce.

Bruce came in to see me as a referral from a co-worker who is already a client of mine. Bruce was 57 ½ years old and wanted to retire from his current job and move to Florida and work part time. His question to me was, "Can I actually do this?" Trying to retire at such a young age creates some interesting challenges. The first question I asked: "What are you going to do for health insurance?" Fortunately, Bruce was able to take his health insurance with him after he left his current job. He would have to pay premiums for the health insurance until he reached age 65 and became eligible for Medicare, but he was insured.

My next area of concern was Bruce's young age of 57. Typically, people roll over their 401(k) to their own IRA to give them more choices for investments and more control over the assets when they retire. The standard rule is you have to be age 59 ½ to do this under the in-service, non-hardship rollover provision that is part of the current tax code. However, there is an exception to this rule — separation of service from your current job. So, in Bruce's case, since he was retiring from his job, he met the separation of service trigger. So far, so good! His dream was closer to being a reality! The next challenge for Bruce was, how could we create income for him? Because he was only 57 ½, he couldn't take withdrawals from his IRA without a pre-59-½ 10 percent early withdrawal penalty from the IRS.

This is where the use of a competent advisor really paid off for Bruce. There is a rule in the tax code that is rarely used but can be very beneficial to those people who are looking to retire at a younger age. It works like this: If you are participating in your company's 401(k) plan and you leave employment in the year you turn 55, or after age 55, you can take income from the 401(k) if you leave it with the company you are separating from without incurring the 10 percent federal penalty on the withdrawals. In Bruce's case, this worked out wonderfully. We left enough money in his 401(k) to give him income for the two years until he reached age 59 ½. The remainder of the 401(k), he rolled over to his IRA. Now, at age 59 ½ he could take income from the IRA without the 10 percent penalty from the IRS.

Bruce also decided to start taking his Social Security benefit at his full retirement age of 67. That Social Security income would allow him to discontinue taking withdrawals from his IRA until he turns 70 ½, which is when the IRS will require that he take a minimum distribution from that account. This will also give him 3 ½ years to let his IRA account grow without being depleted by withdrawals. Needless to say, when I delivered this news to Bruce, he was ecstatic! His dream of retiring at a relatively young age, moving on to part-time work in sunny Florida was coming true!

Bruce's comment to me was, "I am so glad I came to see you. I thought I had saved enough but I wasn't sure if I could really do it, thanks for helping me achieve my dream."

Definitely my pleasure, Bruce.

CHAPTER 9

Let's Create Some Income

I can't stress strongly enough the importance of focusing on building a strong base of income for retirement. In my 30-plus years of experience, the most successful and stress-free retirees I work with are the ones who have built a solid foundation of income.

Let's look at the two most popular ways to create your retirement income.

I refer to the two strategies as the "safe withdrawal rate" and "flooring."

CREATING **RETIREMENT INCOME**

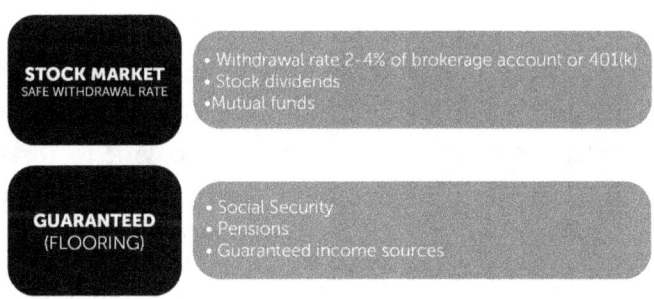

The safe withdrawal rate method uses a *basket* of diversified stocks that the financial broker will try to manage in hopes of earning at least the safe withdrawal rate that they establish in a planning process. Most brokers will use a *Monte Carlo* scenario that looks back over different time periods and establishes a probability, based on using a safe withdrawal rate and using investments that assume a safe withdrawal rate. The entire model is based on the assumption that there is a high probability the retirement assets will last through retirement.

The standard safe withdrawal rate can be around 4 percent, the average rate most financial advisors or brokers are likely to use. In times when there is market turmoil, you will most likely see this rate go down. I have seen some brokers suggest around 2 percent as a safe withdrawal rate to try and protect the portfolio. Generally, your income is set at whatever your portfolio can generate. Let's use the 4 percent rate since that is what is mostly used. For example, if you have $500,000 in your portfolio, at a safe withdrawal rate of 4 percent, your portfolio would be expected to generate about $20,000 per year in income.

There are a couple of different things to consider, though. Suppose a portfolio doesn't earn 4 percent in any given year. Let's assume it only earns 3 percent. The investor or retiree would have to make a choice between receiving $15,000 for that year or continuing to receive the original $20,000 and hoping the portfolio can make up the $5,000 difference the next year. If the portfolio takes a really steep drop and the returns are negative, as we have seen in the past, the investor might have to make a decision between greatly reducing or even suspending payments for a while to try and let the portfolio rebound. Now, if this is your discretionary income, then this scenario could be easy to live with. The problem with that scenario is, most people are setting up their investment portfolio as a necessary part of their income and can't afford to reduce it too much, if at all.

This is also where I again want to caution you about those projected returns that are most likely too high to achieve. I have seen people in my office who are in real danger of running out of money during their retirement. The reason? They really didn't have enough money in their retirement accounts to retire at the level of income they wanted or needed. However, the numbers plugged into a projection gave them their desired income. The problem is, the projected interest was way too high to achieve, at least for the short term, and, with withdrawals coming out for income adding to lower returns or even losses, they were rapidly depleting their retirement account. As you can imagine, this is not a recipe for restful nights once you see your account quickly slipping away and your *goose being cooked*.

If you decide to use the *safe withdrawal rate* retirement strategy, make sure you do so with your eyes wide open. As long as you know the risks and you are comfortable with a wider (realistic) range of projected returns, it may be a strategy you select to provide income that will hopefully last throughout your retirement years.

However, many people do not want the stress of watching the market every day to see if their retirement nest eggs are safe, wondering if their goose will be able to provide the golden eggs of income they need. Fortunately for those people, there are other strategies to consider that might better fit their personalities, needs and desires.

An alternative strategy to the safe withdrawal rate is the *flooring* method.

Flooring might be a good option if you are just a little too nervous using the *safe withdrawal rate* strategy and you want to make sure you have a certain amount of income coming in each year or month, no matter what happens in the stock market. This strategy is for those of you who don't want the daily performance of the stock market to affect the "floor" of income you have built. This is a particularly popular strategy for those people who are not in a position to risk getting less income than they need to make their retirement plans successful. This *floor* of income can also be established with inflation protection features built in to address the risk of decreased purchasing power throughout your retirement years because of inflation.

The *flooring* strategy typically uses a certain percentage of your retirement portfolio to create guaranteed income and invests the remainder of your retirement portfolio for growth and liquidity, and should do this according to your risk tolerance.

Here I would like to remind you that, while planning for income and potential growth in your retirement years is very important, it is equally important to make sure you have enough of your total assets that are truly liquid. By liquid, I mean money that is readily available to you to be used for emergencies or to cover those purchases you didn't plan for. Purchases such as a broken furnace, major appliances, car repairs, etc. This is where I usually see two types of people. Those who believe they need little to no emergency cash available, and those who think they need way too much and they lose potential growth on a large portion of their retirement portfolio. Try to be honest and reasonable when assessing this need, and if you have a financial advisor who does not recommend a comfortable liquid cash amount, you might want to consider getting an opinion from an advisor who works more exclusively with making recommendations for people around retirement who might share your circumstances.

What I like to do with clients is find out what that base number is, that amount of money you need every month to cover those fixed expenses in your budget like the mortgage payment if you have one, vehicle payments, food, clothing, insurance premiums, etc. What is your bottom line number? Once you cover that number with a guaranteed income, you can breathe a little easier.

Using the *flooring* strategy might be the strategy that gives you that goose insurance that helps you rest peacefully at night regardless of what the market is doing in the crazy world we live in. For many people, this is extremely important to them when trying to decide whether they can or want to retire and when.

Most of the clients I work with usually don't use just one or the other of the two strategies, they use a combination of the flooring strategy and the safe withdrawal rate strategy, based on what fits their risk tolerance, to achieve their retirement goals.

QUIZ TIME!

Please take the time to take the quiz. It is included to help you see what you have retained or what you might need to go back and review about retirement income planning. It will hopefully give you confidence to plan a wonderful retirement and sleep restfully at night without worrying about your retirement income.

1.   What is the most significant change that has taken place in pension planning?
2.   Who is responsible for creating your *pension* (your mailbox money) or retirement income plan?
3.   What are typically the two largest paychecks in retirement?
4.   What does ROI mean after retirement?
5.   What is the "Retirement Danger Zone?"
6.   What are "Green Money" assets?
7.   What are "Red Money" assets?
8.   The phase of your life spent preparing your finances for retirement is the _____ phase.
9.   The phase of your financial life once you retire is the _____ phase.
10. What are the two rules of a very successful investor?
    1.
    2.

Answers on page 113.

CHAPTER 10

Leaving a Legacy

We have spent many chapters discussing ways for you to be successful in your retirement years. However, this book would not be complete if I did not talk about what kind of legacy you would like to leave and how you might want to go about accomplishing that. Although I am not an attorney, it is important to discuss wills, trusts and last wishes. In the years I have been in practice, I have witnessed many tragic endings in probate court of what could have been a wonderful legacy, which instead became family fights and near or complete loss of all the assets that were accumulated over a lifetime of hard work and sacrifice.

Depending on the size of your estate, you may want to consider a trust versus a will. That is something you can discuss with a qualified financial advisor who can go over some of the pros and cons of each and who can refer you to a qualified estate planning attorney. I firmly believe that it is quite beneficial to get an attorney who specializes in writing estate planning documents – after all, as with many professions, all attorneys are not created equal. It is very important to have your estate planning documents — such as wills, trusts, powers of attorney, durable medical powers of attorney and living wills — done correctly so they will stand up to any challenges.

Among the many considerations of estate planning, keep in mind that the topmost concern isn't always what tools you use; it's most important that you follow through on whatever it is that you are using. I have seen many clients in my office who, for some reason or other, decided they needed a trust instead of a will. However, after years of having a revocable living trust set up, they still had not funded it. In other words, the revocable trust was an empty shell.

Perhaps a better way to explain this is to give you a picture of what I am talking about. Consider a trust to be like a basket, an empty basket. Everything that you want protected or distributed a certain way after your death needs to be put into that empty basket. That is where many people fall short in their estate planning. While they intend to use a trust, they simply do not complete the process and fund the trust.

I have actually seen people in my office who have had a trust for many years that was never funded at all. They were under the misconception that just because they had a trust document created, they were all set. As you know by now, that is not the case. If the trust is not funded when you die, all of your estate that is outside of the trust will go through probate. After probate, the court may hopefully distribute your assets according to the wishes of your trust. Of course, anything can happen to derail your wishes during the probate process. If you believe you need a trust instead of a will, make sure it is funded.

If you do not need a trust, then you most likely need a will. Again, it is very beneficial to make sure the attorney you use to create your will is experienced in doing so. Try to be as specific and thorough as possible when creating your will. In my practice, I often meet with people who have a will, but it has not been updated for years. In many cases, the will was done when their children where small. Those children are now adults and have children of their own! Time to update. Way past time, actually. As you can imagine, many things may have changed over the years, including the way you want to leave your legacy. It is a good practice to take your will out every few years and re-read it to make sure it still reflects your wishes. If not, update it and then destroy the old will.

You might be amazed to know that many people do not have a will or trust at all. In fact, one June 2016 survey showed that two-thirds of Americans over age 35 don't have wills. Perhaps even more surprisingly, half of Americans older than 65 don't have up-to-date wills or legacy documents![15]

As I mentioned earlier, I see this play out in real life in my office. I have heard reasons such as, "I just can't decide exactly what I want to do or who I want to leave things to," or "I keep saying I have to do that but for some reason I just never get around to it." You can pretty much rest assured that if you do not have a will, what you hope will happen to your estate upon your death will not be what happens. In fact, as in many cases, your estate will be consumed by legal fees. Let me give you a few real life examples of what actually happened to estates without a will.

James and Irene were hard-working farmers. They lived on a 400 acre farm that had been in the family for years. They were not wealthy people in monetary assets, but over the years, because of upscale developments around their home, the property had become quite valuable. However, James and Irene had no intention of selling their farm. The couple had eight children. Irene pre-deceased James when she was 89 and James passed away two years later at the age of 92. They never took the time to create a will. At

---

[15] The U.S. Legal Wills Blog. 2016. "Demystifying the Last Will and Testament: Are there even fewer Americans without Wills?" https://www.uslegalwills.com/ blog/americans-without-wills/. Accessed Jan. 6, 2017.

the time of their death, six children were still alive, however, all eight children had multiple children of their own. The two children that pre-deceased their parents both had three children. At the time of James' death, the land had an appraised value of approximately $820,000.00. That was seven years ago. At this point, the family still can't agree on what to do with the property. It hasn't even been filed in probate because no one in the family will agree to pay the court fees or any fees for an attorney.

Eventually, the homestead was confiscated by the municipality for six years of unpaid property taxes. James and Irene loved their family and they loved their farm. They created many wonderful memories for their children and grandchildren on that farm. I am quite confident that it was not James and Irene's dream to have their cherished farm taken for a few years of unpaid property taxes. Not only was the farm lost, but the once-close family is now bitter, angry and splintered. This all could have been avoided if James and Irene had simply taken the time to create a will or put the land in a trust.

Sadie lived alone in her home that she and her husband had shared for 19 years. Sadie was a widow for approximately 11 years when she met Carl. Sadie and Carl soon became inseparable and decided to get married. They decided to live in Sadie's home. Carl and Sadie were happily married for 34 years when Sadie unexpectedly passed away at the age of 84. Carl and Sadie had never created a will together. Sadie had a will that she had done right after her first husband passed away. In that will, Sadie left her house to her two children.

Sadie's two children lived in other states and both had successful careers. However, when they realized that their mother had not changed or updated her will since marrying Carl and that the house belonged to them, Carl was given a 30-day notice to vacate the premises. The notice arrived via certified mail prior to Sadie's funeral. Carl, who was doing his best to plan his beloved wife's funeral, suddenly found himself homeless.

Within 30 days, Carl had been forced to bury his wife, pack his belongings and move to a small apartment in a nearby town. According to Carl, it was always Sadie's intention and wishes that Carl would live in her home until the day he decided not to or passed away, and *then* the home would go to her children. However, Sadie never updated her will to include those instructions and wishes. A simple review and update of the will would have prevented this tragic outcome for Carl.

Joe and Cindy raised their one and only child, Phil, and then decided to open their home to foster children. One little girl that they took into their home as foster parents became very special to them and they decided to adopt her. They adopted Jenny when she was 14. Jenny was part of their family for the rest of Joe and Cindy's life. In fact, Jenny took care of her adoptive parents when they needed care in their elder years. Phil had moved to a different state many miles away to attend college and decided to live there. Due to the distance, Phil saw his parents only once or twice per year.

Joe and Cindy had a will drawn up when they had their first child, Phil. They never reviewed that will or updated it over the years. When Joe, who was pre-deceased by Cindy, passed away, the will left everything they had to Phil. Phil decided that he would not share with his adoptive sister. With the urging of Joe and Cindy's siblings, Jenny decided to challenge the will in probate court. This estate has been tied up in probate court for more than 12 years. The family home to this day sits empty and dark.

Since I have been in practice for over 30 years, believe me, I could fill this book with probate horror stories due to poor planning or no planning. Please take the time and make sure you have an updated will or updated, funded trust. I'm quite sure you do not want to leave a legacy similar to those I have described.

There are a few other legal documents I believe are a vital part of proper legacy planning.

Let's start with a power-of-attorney document, often referred to as a POA. When planning whom to select to be your power of attorney should you be incapable of making your own decisions, it is important to think of the person whom you literally would trust with your life. A complete POA document should give complete power to your selected person or persons. A good way to think of how powerful this document should be is to think of the person you name as having all the same powers you have yourself. As you can imagine, it is very important to be 100 percent sure about your selection.

The person you select does not have to be a relative; it can be a trusted friend. Let me give you an example where this might be the case for someone. My wife, Lisa, has a dear friend, Faith. They have been close friends for over 40 years. Faith's husband has dementia that unfortunately continues to progress. Faith does not have children. After much thought, Faith asked my wife to be her POA, should she ever need one. Faith has complete confidence that her long-time friend would look out for her best interest in all matters. Many people automatically list their spouse as their POA; however, it is not always possible if your spouse has serious health issues or cognitive impairment. Whoever you decide upon, please keep this in mind, your POA is a document that should be reviewed and updated as needed just like your will or trust.

Another important document to have is a durable medical power of attorney. The person you select will be empowered to make your medical decisions should you be unable to do so. Many times this is the same person as your POA, but not always. You may have a close family member or trusted friend who has specific medical knowledge, such as a doctor or nurse, who you believe would be the best person for the job. Whoever you select, make sure they also have a copy of your health care directive or living will, which leads to the next piece of a good legacy plan.

The final document I also believe to be vital for proper legacy planning is a health care directive or living will. This is the document that will state your wishes should you be faced with an end-of-life situation where you are unable to communicate your wishes at the time. I always caution my clients to thoroughly read these documents before signing, and replace or cross out anything you do not agree with or wish to happen. If you do not have your own living will or health care directive, many hospitals or medical facilities will request you sign one they will provide for you. This is not always the best idea, since much of the time in a situation such as this, you are not able to thoroughly read and consider what you are signing.

I have talked with clients in my office who have the attitude of "just let my family decide at the time." That is putting an extreme burden on those you love. When someone in the family is seriously ill, it is a very emotional and stressful time for their loved ones. The last thing they need to deal with is guessing if they are making the right decisions for end-of-life issues. At least give them peace of mind that they know what your wishes are and can do their best to fulfill them.

Truthfully, by making sure all the documents we have discussed in this chapter are complete and up-to-date, you are giving your loved ones the best gift possible and you are doing all you can to leave behind a great legacy.

Many people make the task of legacy planning much bigger in their minds than it really is. It really does not take a lot of time, and with a properly trained attorney or legal service, it should not be that expensive. What is the point of setting up a great plan for retirement and then cooking your goose so it does not produce a great legacy, as well?

CHAPTER 11

Don't Go It Alone

YOU MIGHT NEED A SHERPA!

D ON'T RETIRE TOO YOUNG! This tip has only a little to do with your financial portfolio, and more to do with your age and our need to have a purpose.

A trend I see in my office is people declaring that they are going to retire at a very young age. Typically this is somewhere between their mid-50s and early 60s. When I ask them what they will do after they retire, they tell me, "nothing." They truly have the attitude they have worked enough in their life and they are "ready to fully retire."

Believe me when I tell you, this is usually a recipe for disaster. Not only does the decision to fully retire too young significantly increase the potential number of years that their retirement incomes must last, there also seems to be a basic need for most of us to have a purpose in life. If we don't do anything in retirement, I think it can be very detrimental to our mental and physical health. In addition to needing a purpose, most people retiring too young are also still in working mode. They simply have not switched their thinking from working and being a consumer to being in retirement mode, where they are trying to preserve their nest egg for living expenses or preventing an early spenddown of their retirement accounts.

I personally have seen the vast majority of my clients who retire too young blow up their retirement income plan by spending their liquid assets, then spending the assets in their growth portfolios, and, finally, some even begin taking withdrawals from the accounts that were set up to provide for their protected retirement income later in life. Believe me when I tell you this trend of spending begins very quickly with many early retirees.

Let's talk about what happened with Bob and Mary Lou. Of course these are fictional names, but the story is factually true. Bob and Mary Lou retired when he was 60 and she was 57. They had a nice retirement nest egg that should have provided them with a comfortable income for the duration of their retirement. In addition to the income plan they set up, they also had a generous liquid account and approximately 40 percent of their retirement portfolio in growth accounts to hopefully keep up with inflation, protecting their future purchasing power.

Bob and Mary Lou's retirement income was more than enough to meet their needs and to live a very comfortable, active lifestyle.

However, Bob and Mary Lou quickly became bored. They had no purpose. They did not do any charitable work or even work part time. They wanted to be fully retired. Within a year, they decided they were going to purchase an RV to do more traveling. They purchased a very expensive RV. They did not want to make monthly payments, so they took a large withdrawal out of the growth portion of their retirement portfolio. At the time, their financial professional informed them that this most likely would have a negative impact on future income for them during their retirement.

However, they were bored and the future seemed like a long time away.

Guess what came with this very expensive RV? A significant increase in their monthly expenses. Something they had not completely planned for. Soon they tired of the RV traveling and decided they would be very happy if they could buy a small cabin on a lake in Maine. They put all their time and effort into finding that little cabin. Once they found their perfect place, they withdrew the rest of their liquid cash and the retirement assets that were in their growth portfolio. Again, a financial professional warned them that this would have a significant negative impact on their retirement plan and income. However, they did not take that advice and purchased the little cabin on the lake.

As you might have already guessed, an additional property meant additional expenses. Very quickly, their retirement income was not enough to pay all their new expenses.

Bob and Mary Lou went from a situation where they could have been very comfortable in retirement to a plan that no longer worked for them.

I wish I could say this is a unique story but, unfortunately, it is very common. I have witnessed an alarming number of people who retire at a young age continue buying as if they were still in the *accumulation phase.* Their purchases are usually large ones for things such as vacation homes, lake homes, RVs, motorcycles, expensive new kitchens and the list goes on and on. The real problem with this is that they are using large amounts of their retirement assets to pay for these items when, if they were still working, they would use their income from employment to pay for these items. They are still in the working, consumer mode. Instead of living within the boundaries of their retirement income, they think of ways to spend their retirement accounts in large lump sums. This could be a recipe for financial disaster for any retirement plan.

If you can retire early, good for you. However, take an honest look at what that retirement will look like. What will you need or what do you think you will need to meet your dreams and goals for a happy retirement? Consider this carefully and talk with your financial advisor about these things before setting up your plan. To be perfectly honest, many people have much more success when they retire at a young age if they work part time somewhere or get involved volunteering with their favorite charity or church. Not only does it give them some extra spending money, more importantly, it gives them a purpose.

It is so important to remember that we have all worked very hard for 30, 40 or even 50 years to accumulate the nest egg that will hopefully turn into the *goose* that will lay those beautiful golden eggs — our retirement income.

Think back again about what we went through when trying to save and accumulate enough to retire. We graduated from school and for most of us, whether we went on to college or not, that was where our work life began. Do you remember that first job? For most of us, our first job was just a stepping stone, but it is where we began to realize why our parents told us that money did not grow on trees!

Hopefully at an early point your working career, you started participating in a 401(k) or 403(b) at work or you started seriously saving in a traditional IRA or Roth IRA outside of work. If you were fortunate, you met the love of your life; got married and had some kids; bought a home; sent the kids to grammar school, middle school, high school and college; maybe even paid for a wedding or two; and, at the same time, tried to save something for yourself for retirement! All this time you were watching that little nest egg, or your little "gosling" grow into a golden goose that one day would start laying the golden eggs that will take care of you in your golden years.

This is why we need to do everything we can to protect our *goose from being cooked* by poor investment decisions, a bad sequence of stock market returns or poor spending decisions. As the old saying goes, *"If you cook the goose ... No more eggs."* What takes us many, many years to save and sacrifice for could be lost in a matter of days, weeks or months, as we've witnessed in the not-too-distant past.

Why do we put so much emphasis on not cooking the goose? Because this goose or pot of money you have accumulated is there to fund all the retirement goals and dreams you have. What are your retirement goals and dreams? What is your "why" you want to retire? Is it travel? Golf? Spending more time with the grandchildren? Volunteering for a charity? What motivates you to save and sacrifice? Think about it. These are the things you are protecting by not cooking the goose.

Do you remember our example of the Retirement Danger Zone? Remember that the mountain used in my example was Mount Everest. One of the most dangerous mountains in the world to climb.

Do you know who the first person recorded to have climbed Mount Everest was? It is recorded that Sir Edmund Hillary was the first person to successfully climb Everest and live to tell the story of his climb.

Did he climb alone? No, he had a Sherpa named Tenzing Norgay with him. He had a guide. Many people believe much of his Everest climbing victory was because of his knowledgeable Sherpa guide. A qualified guide is someone who is very familiar with the territory, who knows all the dangerous spots, and how to avoid the pitfalls during the journey. A qualified guide should be able to successfully get you through the danger zones.

It is also rumored that Sir Edmund Hillary might not have been the first to actually climb to the top of Everest. There were two men, George Mallory and Andrew Irvine, who attempted the climb before Hillary, but they were found frozen to death on the mountain. The last time they were spotted by anyone, they were headed up the mountain close to the summit, but when they were found, they were on the way down. There was no way to prove whether they made it to the top or not.

What did Mallory and Irvine need? That's right, they needed a Sherpa! They needed a guide to help them not only get up the mountain, (the accumulation phase) but also to get them down the mountain, as well (the distribution and protection phase).

If you have the ability to do your own retirement planning, good for you, but if you don't, you might want to seek out an experienced financial advisor to help with the planning process. You might need a guide to help you navigate the pitfalls and dangers while you are on your journey toward and during what we are all striving for … a happy retirement.

Another suggestion that I believe makes for not only a happy retirement but a happy life is: GIVE AWAY 10 PERCENT OF WHAT YOU EARN!

Yes that's right, I said give away 10 percent of what you earn. You're probably thinking that, after all this great financial advice, this guy has totally lost his mind, but hold on!

My wife and I have done this for many years and we are always blessed by it. There is a great satisfaction in seeing someone benefit from you choosing to give away a portion of what you have been blessed with.

I believe that, if you are fortunate to have a job or retirement income, you should give away 10 percent of that income to help someone that is less fortunate or to further a good cause. It is written, "Give and it will be given back to you tenfold, pressed down and overflowing." I'm certainly not saying to give with the expectation of getting something back in return, but if you are charitable-minded, things have a way of coming back around and many times the return is far greater than a monitory return. Many times you will blessed in ways that have a lifelong impact.

Let me share a few stories of how this life philosophy has greatly blessed us personally.

One day my wife received a call from a lady who had been a neighbor of ours years earlier. She was an elderly woman and had a sister who had recently moved to our area. Sophie was extremely worried about her sister and asked if we would be willing to check in on her. You see, Sophie's sister, Rosemarie, lived alone, was completely blind, and also suffered from a form of muscular dystrophy. She was mostly confined to a wheelchair. However, she was a hard worker and made her living by typing medical records in her home.

Rosemarie had recently lost her job. The doctor that Rosemarie typed for took a job with a local hospital and closed his practice. Rosemarie had very little notice and no ability to search for a new job that quickly. She had disconnected her phone to save money and was barely getting by on her very small savings account.

My wife and I had never met Rosemarie but readily agreed to check in on her. What a wonderful woman we quickly got to know. After much coaxing, Rosemarie agreed to tell us how much money she needed just to make it through, month by month. She had carefully figured every penny in her savings account and how long she would be able to pay her bills without having a job. What she had not included in her calculations was food.

Because of our practice of giving away 10 percent, we asked if we could help her at least purchase food until she found new employment. She finally agreed to accept just $100 a month, which she assured us would be plenty to buy her food for the month. We also insisted she have a phone in case of any emergencies.

We gave that precious lady, who became a very dear friend of ours, that monthly gift for about four months until one day, we received a call from Rosemarie. She was very excited as she told us she had found a new job! She was going to be typing for another doctor who had heard what a great job she did. She quickly added that she would no longer need that $100.

Rosemarie worked for that doctor until she retired. Witnessing her positive attitude, and faith in a situation where most of us would have given up, blessed us so very much. Many times when we are having a bad day, we think of how Rosemarie would handle it. It quickly changes our attitudes. We really didn't help

Rosemarie nearly as much as she helped us. The gift of getting to know such an inspirational person has changed our lives in remarkable ways.

Again, I can't stress enough that a successful retirement is not just about your retirement income or how much you have in your retirement accounts. I have mentioned previously that most people need to have a purpose in their lives. For my wife and I, that purpose is to leave this world a little bit better than we found it. At least that is what we strive to do.

Lisa and I do not have children of our own, but we love kids and fully realize they are our future. We have decided to do what we can to influence that future in a positive way. For years, we anonymously paid tuitions for children to attend private Christian schools. These were children who were struggling in public schools for various reasons. We were amazed at the difference it made in the lives of these children. Many of them graduated with full college scholarships. These were kids that would not have had much of a chance of attending college at all, had their paths not been changed.

After witnessing many heartwarming success stories, we decided to start our own 501(c)(3) charitable organization, called Legacy Inc., to enable even more children to have the same chances as the ones we sponsored privately. As I mentioned earlier, one of the ways we help provide funding for this worthy cause is by donating 10 percent of our income.

I wanted to share these few stories with you for the purpose of inspiring you. Once people adopt this attitude, the possibilities of making positive impacts in the world around us are limitless. It is a life philosophy that we hope you consider adopting. It will change your life as well as those you are able to help.

If you can't give away 10 percent, there are other equally important ways to be charitable-minded, such as donating a portion of your time. A worthy cause doesn't have to be a formal charity or church, it can be helping your elderly neighbor mow his grass or shovel her driveway. Taking the time to sincerely thank the person who just handed you your coffee on the go or, in addition to thanking them verbally, tipping them with a $5 or $10 dollar bill at the take-out window. They work hard and it is rewarding to be appreciated for what you do. Complimenting someone who has truly done a good job means the world to them. My wife and I have found just visiting an elderly neighbor or someone who most likely is lonely does them a world of good. You can learn so much by just listening to their stories. You will be amazed at how many heroes who sacrificially served our country live so close to you.

It is my sincerest desire that the information in this book assists you in having a successful, fulfilling retirement. Perhaps you will be better educated and prepared to select the right qualified financial advisor. Remember, if you are not comfortable asking as many questions as you need to understand the recommended plan, you most likely do not have the right financial advisor. For instance, our office works hard as a team to ensure our clients know they are welcome and appreciated, after all, we work for them. My clients often tell me how comfortable they feel in our office, from the inviting, open atmosphere to the friendly staff in the front office who make them feel as important as they are when they arrive for their appointment.

I will conclude by summing it up this way: Throughout my career as a financial advisor, I have found that a happy retirement consists of many aspects. Staying busy and having a true purpose in your life is essential. Doing your best to make wise investment decisions, especially during the danger zone of retirement, is a burden greatly shared if you use a financial Sherpa (a qualified financial advisor) to successfully guide you. However, if you have only retained one bit of wisdom to help you with your retirement planning from reading this book, please let it be this:

Don't cook the goose that lays *your* golden retirement eggs!

ANSWERS

If you didn't take the quizzes in the book, you may go back and take them on pages 67 and 94. If you have already taken the quizzes, the answers are following. Remember to flip back and review any sections where you missed questions or are still uncertain about. Good luck!

Answers to the Social Security quiz:

1. 60
2. Guaranteed, inflation-adjusted, provides lifetime income, tax-preferred
3. 85
4. Full retirement age, primary insurance amount
5. Age 66
6. 41.7

Answers to the retirement income quiz:

1. The change from the pension plan to the 401(k)

2. You are, if you have a 401(k) or other retirement assets and not a pension at work

3. Social Security and the paycheck you can create from other retirement assets such as your 401(k), 403(b), IRA, etc.

4. Reliability of income

5. The last 10 years before retirement and the first 10 years after retirement

6. Green Money assets have some form of principal protection and include financial products such as CDs, annuities, checking accounts and savings accounts.

7. Red Money assets are assets that are at risk in the market, such as stocks, bonds, mutual funds, variable annuities, etc.

8. Accumulation

9. Distribution and protection

10. Warren Buffet is oft-quoted, saying, "Rule No. 1: Don't lose money" and "Rule No. 2: Don't forget Rule No. 1."

About the Author

Scott Carter, RICP®, CRPC®, was born in Bangor, Maine, and has been a lifelong Maine resident. Scott enjoys mostly warm-weather activities such as boating, swimming and riding ATVs.

"Since the winters can be very long here in Maine, I like to escape some of it by going to Florida and working with my 'snow bird' clients while I am there," he says.

For more than 35 years, Scott has specialized in providing planning and guidance for those who are seeking a better lifestyle in retirement. Whether you have a retirement nest egg of $5 million or $50,000, he can help you make sure it works as hard and as smart as you did in earning and saving it. Your retirement could last as long as 30 years, and you simply cannot afford to make mistakes with your retirement money and run the risk of ruining your lifestyle during your leisure years.

As Scott says, "I have helped literally several hundred individuals and couples, at all economic levels, to enjoy a worry-free retirement knowing that their money is safeguarded, plus working hard and smart, and ready for them when needed."

There is no one "best place" to put your retirement money because each individual and couple has unique requirements, different tolerances for risk and need their money at different times. Likewise, there is no one place to keep your money that fits everyone for exactly the same reasons. In order to make sure your money is in the best place for *you*, your unique circumstances must be taken into consideration. This is where Scott can be of most service.

He says the two most common money mistakes made by the retirement-minded are (a) putting all their retirement assets in short-term savings places, and (b) unknowingly taking risks they can't afford. If you have your retirement money in highly liquid places that allow you access immediately, you're paying a dear price for liquidity you don't need. Not all of your retirement money will be needed at the same time; therefore, you may need to space your investments so they come due when needed, yet retain enough flexibility to take care of an emergency should one arise. Far too many people have all their retirement money in the market, exposed to the risk of principal loss. Certainly some of your money needs to be in short-term places that give you access without penalty. Some may be able to afford the risk of the market with some of their retirement money, and some may prefer products that are less liquid but carry more safety and don't put their principal at risk. Balance is key; too much money in either place is generally a bad plan.

Scott routinely helps people deploy their retirement money properly, meeting their liquidity needs and making sure their risk is suitable, while at the same time helping them strike a proper balance between the short-term and the longer-term maturities. He also helps his clients plan to pay their fair share of taxes — and not one cent more! Scott aims to help his clients coordinate the income from their retirement money, pension (if they have one) and Social Security to assure them a retirement without fear of running out of money in their lifetimes.

For the opportunity to discuss your retirement plans or learn firsthand how Financial Security Alliance may benefit you, contact him at 207-862-2196 or scarter@brookstoneadvisor.com, or visit https://fsaincomesolutions.com. There is no cost or obligation to speak with Scott by phone or for meeting to discuss your circumstances and your retirement plans.

"If I can't be of service, you will at least have the comfort of knowing that you have consulted with a knowledgeable professional about the most important financial decisions in your life. It is very important for you to get retirement 'right,' because there is no second chance. I look forward to working with you soon to help you lower your stress and worry over your retirement years," Scott says.

Scott is a licensed Series 65 Investment Advisor Representative for Brookstone Capital Management and is licensed by the states of Maine, South Carolina, Florida and Tennessee for insurance-related products. Scott is a founding member and is on the board of Legacy Inc., a nonprofit corporation that raises money to help pay tuition for children to attend private Christian schools.

LISA CARTER

Lisa manages Financial Security Alliance's very busy retirement income planning office and has been licensed with the state of Maine for insurance-related products for over 20 years. She is involved in the majority of operations of the business, from client communications to case design.

Lisa also has served on the finance board for approximately 10 years for one of the major hospitals in central Maine.

She is a former Maine legislator, where she served on the banking and finance committee. Lisa remains heavily involved in Maine political issues on the local, state and national level.

As a founding member of Legacy Inc., a 501(c)3 charitable corporation that raises money to help pay tuition for children to attend private Christian schools, Lisa devotes much of her time to the charity, for which she also serves as president of the board.

ACKNOWLEDGMENTS

While it is very hard to thank everyone who has had a hand in this effort, I want to thank a few special people that made this book possible.

First, I want to thank God. I have come to learn that through Him all things are possible.

Second, I want to thank all the clients I have been privileged to work with over the years, many of you have also become dear friends along the way. Thank you for the trust and confidence you have placed in me, it really means a lot.

Next, I want to thank all the teachers and mentors who have helped shape my investment philosophy and have taught me how to pass the knowledge on to those who have been able to benefit from it.

Without a doubt, I saved the best for last. I want to thank my wife, Lisa. Without your assistance and patience, this book would not have been written. You are the best wife and partner I could have ever dreamed of having.

You are my dream come true, I love you.

www.ingramcontent.com/pod-product-compliance
Lightning Source LLC
Chambersburg PA
CBHW070031210526
45170CB00012B/535